Phil and Fern's Family Food

Phil and Ferns Family Food

Phil Vickery

and Fern Britton

GRANADA

First published in Great Britain in 2003
By Granada Media, an imprint of Andre Deutsch Limited
20 Mortimer Street
London W1T 3JW

Recipes © Phil Vickery, 2003

This Morning is a Granada Television Production for itv1

The right of Phil Vickery and Fern Britton to be identified as
the authors of this work has been asserted by them in
accordance with the Copyright, Designs and Patents Act
1988

A catalogue record is available from the British Library

ISBN 0 233 05084 1

Printed and bound in Great Britain

2 4 6 8 10 9 7 5 3 1

Contents

Introduction

Welcome to **Phil and Fern's Family Food**. It's no secret that I love to cook, but with a professional chef in the house, it's difficult getting into the kitchen, let alone cooking a meal. So I must admit that, generally, I only manage to cook a couple of times a week – that's not including the baby food, which for some reason, Phil is happy to leave to me!

People do envy me, living with a professional chef, and it is fantastic. But despite the fact that Phil is always experimenting in the kitchen, I have to make sure that there are plenty of tins of tomatoes, sweetcorn, pasta and rice in the cupboard so I can always knock up a quick meal in case he has decided to cook one of his offal dishes, or some obscure seafood – there are some fish that should definitely be left in the sea! And if for some reason I can't find the necessaries for a quick pasta dish, there is always my favourite bacon sandwiches and fried eggs – very naughty, but so delicious – and the children don't complain either.

Cooking for children can be difficult, but one thing I've learned over the years is that if you keep it simple, then it usually works. It's certainly been true of me. My favourite dishes are generally ones that my mother cooked for me, like roast lamb chops, mint sauce and roast potatoes. Heaven! Phil cooks this for me a lot because he knows how much I love it (check out page 74). Cottage pie is another firm family favourite and one I know most children love. There is room for more adventurous dishes of course, and I think there are some wonderful recipes in this book which should appeal not only to children, but also to adults. For example, the asparagus and chicken lasagne. Everybody loves lasagne, and the asparagus and chicken give it that slightly more sophisticated twist which can make it a perfect dish to cook when friends come to lunch with their children.

As any parent knows, catering for a party of adults is a piece of cake compared to the traumas of cooking for a children's party. The most successful dish I've ever made is a web jelly for a Hallowe'en party, it went down a treat. And there are loads more ideas like that in the Family Feasts and Celebration chapter.

Of course, things don't always turn out the way you want them to. The first time I made scrambled eggs for Phil, I was so nervous that I overcooked them. I ended up serving a plate of rather nasty egg marbles, but he ate it without a murmer. Needless to say, my scrambled egg recipe hasn't made it into this book, but there are plenty of wonderful ideas that I hope you will find as delicious as we do and many of them require less than half an hour to make.

As a busy parent, I know how hard it can be to make sure your children eat well, but the best advice I can give you is always make more than you need and build up a freezer full of your family's favourite food. Children can be fussy and when they are being particularly difficult, the temptation to make your life easier and let them eat chips is strong, especially if you're very busy. So having portions of their favourite food readily available in the freezer can solve arguments and ensure that they eat a nutritious meal with the minimum amount of fuss.

I do hope you find our book useful and inspiring. These recipes have stood us in good stead and we have enjoyed eating every single one of them.

Good luck and bon appetit!

Fern
X

Lunch, Anyone?

Lunch shouldn't be a rushed affair, something you slap together in order to provide your body with fuel. In fact, as with all meals, you should take the time to enjoy the act of eating, even if you only have half an hour to do so. Not only is it easy to put together a tempting meal for the midday repast, but also it needn't be something that takes you half the day to prepare. So, whether sitting down to lunch with family or with friends, or just enjoying a meal for two, you can make it an occasion to savour and enjoy – and all in a very short space of time.

SERVES	PREP	COOK
2	**20** MINS	**10** MINS

Red Cabbage and Chicory Salad with Steamed Chicken

Perhaps surprisingly, red cabbage makes a great salad, as long as it is marinated first. And, although chicken is used here, any steamed meat accompanies this salad perfectly. It is best if you marinate it overnight and adjust the seasoning just before serving.

2 medium corn-fed chicken breasts, skin and fat removed, but with the first wing bone left on

225 g/8 oz red cabbage, very finely sliced (best on a Japanese mandolin)

1 bulb Belgian chicory, very finely sliced (again best on a mandolin)

a little extra virgin olive oil

Dressing

2 tbsp Dijon mustard

2 cloves garlic, finely chopped

3 tbsp extra virgin olive oil

2 tbsp sunflower oil

1 tbsp walnut oil

3 good pinches caster sugar

salt and freshly ground black pepper

1 To make the dressing, place the mustard, garlic, sugar and salt and pepper to taste in a small bowl, and mix well.

2 Gradually add the olive, sunflower and walnut oils, and pour over the cabbage and chicory. Toss thoroughly.

3 Cover and leave to marinate for at least 2 hours or, if possible and even better, overnight.

4 Steam the chicken until cooked, about 8–10 minutes. Cut into slices about 1/2 cm (1/4 in) thick, and serve on a bed of marinated cabbage with a little extra olive oil drizzled over the breast.

Salad Niçoise

Probably the best known of all French salads, salad niçoise is a classic southern French dish filled with flavour.

head of cos (romaine) lettuce, chopped

1 large potato, boiled in its skin, cooled, peeled and cubed

4 ripe plum tomatoes, cut into chunks

4 hard-boiled eggs, peeled and cut into quarters

175 g/6 oz cooked green beans

1 x 200 g/7 oz tin tuna, drained

16 black olives, pitted

10 anchovy fillets

4 tbsp freshly chopped parsley

Dressing

1 tsp Dijon mustard

3 tbsp sherry vinegar

4 tbsp olive oil

2 tbsp sunflower oil

freshly ground black pepper

1 To make the dressing, put the mustard in a bowl, add the vinegar and pepper to taste, and combine well.

2 Gradually add the oils, combining thoroughly as you do so. Just whisk the olive oil and vinegar – don't worry about homogenizing.

3 Place all the ingredients in a large serving bowl or on a platter, taking care to break up the tuna carefully.

4 Pour over the dressing and toss everything together. Serve at once.

Pan-fried Pork Loin and Roast Fennel Salad with Lime Dressing

The dressing for this salad is made from the oil in which the fennel is cooked. This not only utilizes all the olive oil, but also makes a very nice lightly fennel-flavoured dressing. Do remember not to overcook the pork, and use British pork, preferably organic, for a deeper flavour.

2 bulbs fennel, halved lengthways, then cut into 3 or 4 long slices

75 ml/2½ fl oz olive oil, plus extra for cooking

4 sprigs fresh rosemary

2 sprigs fresh thyme

3 cloves garlic, left whole, plus 1 extra, halved

2 pork loin steaks

1 tbsp vegetable oil

salt and freshly ground black pepper

rocket, watercress and lamb's lettuce to serve

Lime Dressing

½ tsp chopped fresh green chilli

2 tsp Dijon mustard

juice of 1 lime

pinch of sugar

1 Place the fennel on a baking tray, spoon over the olive oil, rosemary, 3 cloves garlic and plenty of salt and pepper. Cover with foil and place on the hob. Heat through then cook in a preheated oven at 190°C (375°F, Gas mark 5) for 30–40 minutes, or until the fennel is tender. Do not overcook. Remove from the oven and drain the fennel well in a colander, reserving the oil, then cool completely.

2 To make the dressing, put the chilli, mustard and lime juice into a bowl (if you own a pestle and mortar, this is ideal to crush the chilli). Add a little sugar and mix together well. Gradually add the strained olive oil from the fennel and whisk well so that the dressing emulsifies. Adjust the seasoning and reserve.

3 Meanwhile, season the pork well with salt and pepper, and rub with the extra garlic. Heat a frying or griddle pan and spoon a little vegetable oil over the chops. Cook the pork in the griddle pan for about 8 minutes, or until cooked through, turning over after 3–4 minutes. Try to get a nice colour on the steaks, but do not overcook. Keep warm.

4 Remove the herbs and garlic from the fennel, heat a little extra olive oil in a frying pan until hot, add the reserved fennel slices and brown lightly. Take care, as they will burn quickly (the natural sugars in the fennel concentrate with the slow cooking).

5 To finish, slice the pork into six or seven pieces. Using 2 plates, arrange a couple of fennel slices on each one, top with slices of pork and salad leaves, then alternate with more fennel, salad leaves and pork. Drizzle over a little of the dressing.

6 Eat warm with a few boiled potatoes cooked in a little mint and sea salt. A nice glass of chilled Pinot Grigio is perfect with this salad.

Chicken Patties and Roasted Corn Salsa

This is great brunchy-type food, tasty and interesting, and it also works well served on tortillas as a snack. Children seem to love these recipes. In fact, I've incorporated them into a kid's party, where they went down very well. Some kids even like the touch of chilli used in the salsa, believe it or not.

Chicken Patties with Raisins and Sage	Avocado and Roasted Corn Salsa
500 g/1 lb chicken mince	2 tbsp vegetable oil
1 large egg white	2 cobs sweetcorn, ears removed and
2 tbsp raisins	kernels sliced off
2 tbsp natural yoghurt	$1/2$ tsp ground cumin
zest of 1 lemon	touch of freshly chopped chilli (optional)
1 tbsp finely chopped fresh sage	2 ripe avocados, peeled and scooped
a little vegetable oil for frying	into small pieces
salt and freshly ground black pepper	1 clove garlic, crushed
	juice of 1 large lime
	1 tbsp olive oil
	salt and freshly ground black pepper

1 Place all the ingredients for the chicken patties except the oil into a bowl. Season well with salt and pepper. Mix well and form into 20 small balls, then flatten slightly.

2 Cook the patties in a nonstick frying pan with about 1 teaspoon oil for 3–4 minutes on each side, or until nicely coloured and cooked through.

3 To make the salsa, heat the vegetable oil in a wok or frying pan until quite hot. Add the sweetcorn, cumin and chilli, if using. Cook, sizzling, for a couple of minutes until the corn is slightly golden, then spoon into a bowl.

4 Add the avocado, garlic, lime juice, olive oil, salt and pepper, and mix well.

5 Serve with hot or cold meats and grilled salmon or monkfish. The chicken patties can be served either hot or cold – it's up to you.

Quick Chickpea Soup with Ham and Olive Oil

I think that certain tinned pulses are extremely good in soups and stews – split peas, haricot beans and borlotti beans, for example. Dried beans are fine, but you have to soak them overnight and cook them properly. This can be a bit of a pain, although, if you do have the time, try them. I once cooked this soup for a very well known chef/writer some years ago. He liked it so much that he had two bowls. So, there you go – it must be good.

4 tsp vegetable oil

2 small onions, chopped

1 small leek, chopped, rinsed well and drained

2 garlic cloves, crushed

about 1.2 litres (2 pints) hot chicken or vegetable stock

2 x 410 g (14 oz) tins chickpeas, drained

pinch of medium curry powder

2 tsp fresh thyme leaves

200 g/7 oz chopped ham off the bone

dash of milk (optional)

salt and freshly ground black pepper

olive oil to drizzle

1 Heat the vegetable oil in a large pan, then add the onion, leek and garlic, and cook gently until they are tender and golden brown – but do not allow to burn. Add the stock, chickpeas, curry powder and thyme. Simmer for 15–20 minutes, or until all the vegetables are soft and tender.

2 Pour the soup into a blender, reserving about a third of the cooked chickpeas and a few pieces of onion. Whizz until smooth – you may need to do this in batches – then pour back into the pan, check the seasoning and add a little milk if the soup is too thick. Add the reserved chickpeas and onion, and the ham, and warm through.

3 Serve piping hot, with a little olive oil drizzled over the top and stirred in.

Japanese Miso Soup with Wasabi

This soup is incredibly tasty and packed full of flavour, and many variations of miso are made and consumed in Japan. The soup must be eaten piping hot and from small bowls so that it keeps its heat. The addition of a little wasabi is my idea and not strictly correct, but it does give the soup a nice definition.

Miso is fermented soya bean paste and is made by boiling soya beans, mashing them, then adding rice or barley. The fermentation takes place as a result of the introduction of a yeast. And very tasty it is, too.

1 small carrot, peeled and cut into perfect $1/2$ cm/$1/4$ in cubes	1 tbsp rice vinegar
	3–4 tbsp dark soy sauce
about 2 tbsp miso paste (available from supermarkets either ready to use or as a dried instant powder)	2 tsp wasabi (available from supermarkets or Japanese food stores)
125 g/4 oz firm tofu, cut into $1/2$ cm/$1/4$ in cubes	3 spring onions, thinly sliced on a slight angle
	touch of freshly ground black pepper

1 Place the carrot, 1 litre ($1^3/4$ pints) water and miso paste into a saucepan. Bring to the boil, then turn down the heat and simmer for 4 minutes.

2 Next add the tofu, rice vinegar, soy sauce and wasabi. Cook for a further minute, being careful to keep the tofu in nice pieces.

3 Add a touch of pepper and ladle the soup into small bowls. Top with the spring onion and serve at once. Simple and very refreshing.

Herb Stock with Spring Onions and Olive Oil

A cleansing, tasty, simple soup perfect for the new year. Just make sure that the herbs are added right at the last minute so that they keep their flavour.

600 ml/1 pint strong vegetable stock	4 tbsp roughly chopped fresh parsley,
4 spring onions, thinly sliced on an angle	tarragon, chervil, basil and coriander
1 large carrot, peeled and cut	4 tbsp extra virgin olive oil
into small cubes	salt and freshly ground black pepper

1 Place the stock into a small saucepan and bring to the boil.

2 Reduce the heat and simmer very gently, adding the carrot and cooking for 5–7 minutes. Add the spring onion and simmer for a further minute.

3 Remove from the heat and add the herbs, salt, pepper and olive oil. Stir through gently.

4 Serve piping hot and straight away, with crusty French bread or crackers.

Steamed Clams and Prawns with White Wine and Parsley

This dish can be a bit pricey, but it is well worth the expense. It has a clean, powerful flavour and is healthy and light, making for a great summer lunch dish.

1 glass medium dry white wine	2 rashers back bacon, with all fat removed, finely diced
1 clove garlic, crushed	
2 small shallots, finely chopped	2 heaped tbsp freshly chopped flat-leaf parsley
2 tbsp olive oil	
1.5 kg/3 lb large clams, well scrubbed	2 heaped tbsp freshly chopped tarragon
	squeeze of lemon juice
8 tiger prawns, peeled and deveined	salt and freshly ground black pepper

1 Place the white wine in a medium saucepan, and add the garlic, shallot, olive oil, salt and pepper. Bring to the boil and drive off the alcohol.

2 Add the clams, prawns and bacon, stir well and cover the pan with a tight-fitting lid. Cook for 4–5 minutes.

3 Remove the lid from the pan – the aroma will be gorgeous and the clams should all be open. A bad clam is fairly easy to spot – discard any that float, are open or feel very light in weight. All shellfish should smell fresh and not fishy. Check and adjust seasoning if necessary.

4 Add the parsley, tarragon and squeeze of lemon. Stir well, pile into bowls and tuck in. You can serve with fresh, crusty bread to mop up juices.

Flat Mushroom 'Buns'

I modelled this idea on a burger bun. The secret is to ensure that all the flat mushrooms are the same size and cut everything to fit in the bun so that when it's finally chilled it will look very impressive. Flat mushrooms are very good value for money.

8 medium flat mushrooms

4 tbsp olive oil

8 slices Port Salut cheese, about
$1/2$ cm/$1/4$ in thick

4 slices ham cooked on the bone, sliced

2 ripe beef tomatoes

about 2 tbsp English mustard

4 leaves fresh basil

salt and freshly ground black pepper

1 Cut the stalks out of the mushrooms and season well with salt and pepper. Drizzle over the olive oil and cook under a preheated grill at its hottest setting for 5–6 minutes each side. Be careful not to overcook. Allow to cool slightly.

2 Take a plain cutter the same size as the flat mushrooms, then cut the ham and cheese to the same circumference as the flat mushrooms. Slice the tomatoes into roughly the same size.

3 Place a mushroom open side up on a chopping board. Top with a layer of ham, season well with salt and pepper and a touch of mustard. Next add further layers of cheese, then tomato, seasoning as you go. Finally add the basil leaf and top with another flat mushroom. Continue until you have used all the mushrooms.

4 Press lightly, wrap each 'bun' in cling film and chill overnight. To eat, cut each mushroom bun in half and skewer with fancy cocktail sticks.

Pork with Lemon Thyme and Sichuan Pepper

Lean pork makes very good kebab-style food. It's quite difficult to form onto skewers on its own, so I have added a little egg white – great protein with no fat. The coupling of dried fruits and couscous is not a new one. A lot of North African food combines the two. The secret is to season the couscous well – there is nothing worse than insipid couscous.

400 g/14 oz lean pork mince	**Couscous**
2 tbsp fresh lemon thyme or freshly grated lemon zest	110 g/4 oz couscous
	200 ml/7 fl oz strong chicken stock, boiling
1 tsp crushed Sichuan pepper	50 g/2 oz ready-to-eat dried peaches
1 egg white	or apricots, finely chopped
2 tbsp dried breadcrumbs (optional)	2 tbsp virgin olive oil
2 tsp vegetable oil	juice of 1/2 lime
sea salt and freshly ground black pepper	salt and freshly ground black pepper

1 Place the pork in a bowl and mix in the lemon thyme, Sichuan pepper, salt, pepper and egg white. Make sure that you mix everything together well. You can add a few dried breadcrumbs if you want to tighten up the mixture. Remember, the more breadcrumbs you add, the dryer the kebabs will be, so take care. Marinate for at least 30 minutes or overnight in the refrigerator.

2 Place the couscous into a bowl. Pour on the boiling stock, season well with salt and pepper, add the peaches, cover and leave for 20 minutes.

3 Meanwhile, mould the marinated pork onto kebab skewers, and cook in a preheated, sizzling nonstick griddle pan, lightly oiled with the vegetable oil, for 6–8 minutes. Keep turning so that the pork cooks and browns evenly. Add the olive oil and lime juice to the couscous and stir well.

4 To serve, spoon the couscous onto a plate and top with the cooked pork. I sometimes serve this with a fruity Indian condiment – mango chutney or, best of all, mango and yoghurt dip.

SERVES	PREP	COOK
2	**15** MINS	**35** MINS

Vegetable Soup with New Potatoes and Lemon Sole

Steaming is a very healthy way of cooking and keeps all the wonderful flavours in the pot. It has become very trendy over the past couple of years and also saves on energy. This particular idea is a great one for a couple wanting an easy, healthy lunch and is very simple indeed. The foods to be steamed can vary greatly, so go on, experiment.

1 small parsnip, chopped	600 ml/1 pint vegetable stock, boiling
1 small carrot, chopped	300 g/10 oz baby new potatoes
1 red onion, chopped	2 medium lemon sole fillets,
2 cloves garlic, finely chopped	about 85 g/3 oz each, skinned
small handful of curly kale leaves,	salt and freshly ground
roughly chopped	black pepper

1 Place the parsnip, carrot, onion, garlic and curly kale in the bottom of a steamer. Add the boiling stock, season well and bring to the boil.

2 Top the boiling vegetables with the steamer tray. Pop in the new potatoes and put on the lid. Reduce the heat and simmer gently for about 30 minutes. Make sure that the soup does not boil too rapidly, and take care to ensure the lid is on tightly, so that all the moisture stays inside the cooker. Top up with boiling stock if needed.

3 After about 30 minutes, pierce the potatoes to see if they are cooked. If they are, add the top pan and the lemon sole, placed on lightly buttered foil, on top of the potatoes. Season well, put the lid back on and cook for a further 20 minutes, or until the sole is lightly cooked. Times will vary, so just use your common sense.

4 That's it. Simply serve the soup separately, with the sole and potatoes as a main course, perhaps accompanied with a little salsa verde or tartar sauce.

Bacon, Potato and Savoy Cabbage Layer Cake

Most Irish food comes back to bacon, potato or cabbage in one guise or another. These three ingredients are really the bedrock of Irish food. Over the centuries, there have been thousands of recipes invented using these staples, along with lamb (Irish stew) and cheese. These days, there are some fantastic varieties of cheese available – Coolea, Gubbeen and Milleen to name but three. Boxty, or rasp, is another Irish classic, a sort of pancake-come-muffin, invented to eke out potatoes during the great potato famine of 1841. You can use any main crop potato for this recipe, but not new potatoes, which are unsuitable.

25 g/1 oz unsalted butter	600 g/1 lb 5 oz medium potatoes, peeled and sliced extremely thinly (on a mandolin is ideal)
1 tbsp olive oil	
1/2 small savoy cabbage, inner leaves only, very finely sliced	200 g/7 oz Coolea, Cheddar or Gubbeen cheese, finely grated
3–4 tbsp vegetable oil	
200 g/7 oz streaky bacon, chopped	salt and freshly ground black pepper

1 Heat the butter and olive oil together in a pan. Add the cabbage and cook, uncovered, for about 15 minutes until softened. Drain well in a colander.

2 Add the vegetable oil to a separate pan, heat and cook the bacon until it has taken just a little colour and the fat runs. Drain off the bacon in a colander, reserving the fat.

3 Place the cabbage in a bowl and add the hot bacon. Mix well.

4 Toss the potato in the reserved bacon fat, then place a layer of potato in the bottom of an oiled nonstick frying pan, overlapping the pieces. (If you don't have an ovenproof frying pan, a small square or round baking tray or ovenproof dish can be used instead.) Season with a little salt and pepper, spread on a little cabbage and bacon, then top with some cheese. This helps to keep the whole cake together. Continue overlapping the potatoes, layering with cabbage and bacon, and seasoning as you go.

5 Place the pan on the stove and heat for a few seconds so that the potato starts to brown and bubble.

6 Cover lightly with foil and bake in the preheated oven at 200°C (400°F, Gas mark 6) for about 50 minutes. When cooked, remove the foil – you should be able to pierce the cake with a knife with no resistance.

7 Cool, then turn out onto a chopping board, cut into wedges and serve with a few salad leaves dressed with a little sherry vinegar dressing.

Swede and Sweetcorn Chowder with Parsley Oil

Many years ago, I worked with a French chef who thought that parsnips, swedes and turnips should only be fed to cattle and pigs. When I challenged him about this sweeping condemnation, all he could say was that they had no flavour. Over the next few months, I set about cooking all sorts of different dishes including roasted parsnips with honey and swede and bacon soup. He would eat away, trying to hold back exactly what he thought. In the end, he was forced to concede that they were very good, but he also said that it would never catch on in France. I find this amazing. Here is a country that brought the cooking world gizzard salad, frogs' legs, chicken cooked in a pig's stomach and foie gras, to name just a few, but cannot come to grips with a wonderful flavour such as a swede or parsnip. Well, it's their loss.

2 tbsp olive oil
15 g/¹/₂ oz unsalted butter
2 small onions, roughly chopped into 1 cm/¹/₂ in pieces
450 g/1 lb swede, skin carefully removed and cut into 1 cm/¹/₂ in cubes
1–2 tbsp plain flour
1 clove garlic, crushed
about 600 ml/1 pint strong vegetable stock, boiling

1 x 285 g/9 oz tin sweetcorn kernels, well drained
salt and freshly ground black pepper
Parsley Oil
15 g/¹/₂ oz curly parsley, stalks removed
3 tbsp virgin olive oil

1 Heat the oil and butter together in a sauté pan or casserole dish. When the butter is starting to brown, add the onion and swede, and cook for 4–5 minutes, stirring occasionally, until the onion starts to colour.

2 Add the flour and soak up all the oil and butter. Next, add the garlic and vegetable stock. Bring to the boil, stirring continuously, and adjust the seasoning as needed. You need to end up with a not-too-thick stew. If the liquor is a little too thick, then add a touch more stock.

3 When simmering, cover with a tight-fitting lid and place into a preheated oven at 160°C (325°F, Gas mark 4), and cook for 35–40 minutes, or until the swede is soft but not falling apart. Remove from the oven and allow to cool – cooling and reheating the chowder increases its flavour.

4 Making the parsley oil is a very simple task: just pop the parsley into a liquidizer or blender, and add the olive oil. Whizz until the oil turns a beautiful green – you may need to add a little more oil – then strain through a fine sieve and keep at room temperature until needed.

5 To serve, reheat the chowder in a shallow pan, add the sweetcorn at the last minute to just warm through, otherwise the kernels will toughen and lose all their sweetness. Spoon into large bowls, and drizzle a tablespoon or so of parsley oil over each serving.

Super Juices

I was given a juicer for Christmas a few years ago and really didn't do much with it for ages. It just stayed in the cupboard. That was until we stayed with Nick and Holly Nairn last year. Holly made us wonderful juices for breakfast every day and they were fantastic. So give these a whirl – they are delicious.

Green Apple with Mint and Lime
8 Granny Smith apples
juice of 1 large lime
10 fresh mint leaves
6 ice cubes

Carrot, Beetroot, Orange and Chilli
4 large carrots
4 medium beetroot
2 large oranges
1 small fresh red chilli
4 stalks celery
a little celery salt

Red Grapefruit, Pineapple and Honey
1 medium sweet pineapple
2 pink grapefruit
2 tablespoons runny honey

1 What could be simpler? Just add the ingredients for the respective juice to the juicer and turn into a smooth purée. You don't even need to peel the fruit and vegetables. There you are – fresh-made heaven.

2 You can use a blender if you don't have a juicer, but the resulting purée won't be as smooth and velvety.

SERVES 4-6 **PREP 15 MINS** **COOK 5 MINS**

Summer Pudding

There really is no great secret to summer pudding. The key is balance: not too much sugar and a little lemon juice. Defrosted frozen currants are fine, even though purists will be up in arms, but you must use fresh strawberries and raspberries. Some people say that you should not use strawberries at all. My answer to that is 'Rubbish!' They are *the* summer fruit, along with raspberries.

250 g/8 oz redcurrants, blackcurrants or whitecurrants, or a mixture, stalks removed, plus extra redcurrants, to decorate

250 g/8 oz fresh raspberries

250 g/8 oz strawberries

juice and zest of a large lemon

120 g/4 oz granulated sugar

6 slices medium-sliced white bread, crusts removed

a little caster sugar, to decorate

double cream, lightly whipped, to serve

1 Cut the bread to fit in a 16 cm x 10 cm (6 in x 4 in) deep pudding basin, leaving one slice for the top. Do not be too worried about the appearance – just make sure that they overlap, then press them lightly to the bowl.

2 Place the currants, strawberries and raspberries in a saucepan. Add the sugar and lemon juice. Bring to the boil, stirring occasionally – try not too break up the fruit too much. Once boiling, remove from the stove immediately and cool slightly. The fruit must not be overcooked.

3 Pour into the prepared bowl and top with the last piece of bread. Cover with a layer of cling film, then a saucer to fit inside the bowl and a heavy weight. Refrigerate for at least 4 hours – overnight is best.

4 Carefully remove the pudding from the bowl. Decorate with a few strings of redcurrants rolled in caster sugar and placed on top, and serve with a *very* large bowl of lightly whipped double cream.

Note: Don't worry too much about any blotches of unsoaked bread. If you really want to, you can paint with a little blackcurrant juice using a pastry brush, or pour over some soft fruit sauce made by blending fresh fruits and a little sugar, water and lemon juice. Slightly overripe fruit is perfect for this.

Strawberry and Hazelnut Shortcake

Strawberries and hazelnuts seem to work very well indeed. If you want to be really posh, you can roast the nuts in a moderate oven first, then roll them in a tea towel to remove the skins. Or just roughly chop them in a food processor and add uncooked. It really is up to you. Make sure that you chill the shortbread completely before attempting to roll – it will make the job much easier.

Always buy English strawberries – they are the best by far. Just remember the smell test: pick up the punnet and, if there is a wonderful aroma of sweet strawberries, then 99 per cent of the time they will be perfect. No aroma, don't buy! Also, always wash the fruit before 'hulling', as this prevents the strawberry filling with water and becoming soggy.

500 g/1 lb fresh English strawberries, hulled

caster sugar

freshly squeezed lemon juice

touch of cold water

225 ml/8 fl oz double cream, very lightly whipped

icing sugar for dusting

For the Base

175 g/6 oz cold unsalted butter, cut into small cubes

125 g/4 oz caster sugar

225 g/8 oz plain flour (do not use bread flour, as this will make the shortbread tough)

175 g/6 oz hazelnuts, chopped

1 To make the base, place the cold butter and sugar into a mixer and beat until soft and slightly creamy. Do not overbeat.

2 Add the flour and hazelnuts (cooled if you have roasted them), and mix into a firm dough. Wrap in cling film and chill well for 30 minutes.

3 Next, pick out half of the nicest-shaped strawberries and reserve for decorating. Pop the others into a blender or liquidizer, and blitz until smooth with a little sugar, lemon juice and water, until you have a nice thick sauce.

I have left the quantities out on purpose, as it's really up to you. Push the sauce through a fine sieve and adjust the taste – do not oversweeten. Chill well while cooking the shortcake.

4 Cut the shortbread dough into 2 pieces and place one back in the refrigerator. Gently knead the other piece until it is slightly soft, then roll out to about 1/2 cm (1/4 in) thick on a lightly floured board or work surface. Cut into 4 large circles using a pastry cutter (an inverted tea cup is also a good size). Carefully lift and place on a baking sheet.

5 Bake in a preheated oven at 190°C (375°F, Gas mark 5) for 15–20 minutes until slightly browned. Repeat the process with the other piece of shortcake, so that you end up with 8 lightly cooked discs. Cool completely.

6 The next part is the simplest. Lay 4 shortcake discs onto 4 plates. Arrange the reserved strawberries on top – you may need to slice some. Spoon over a large dollop of whipped cream and a little strawberry sauce. Top each one with the other 4 discs of shortbread and dust with icing sugar.

7 Serve straight away with extra strawberry sauce.

SERVES
4

PREP
15
MINS

COOK
10
MINS

Warm Strawberry and Orange Pancakes

The less that you do with perfectly ripe, gorgeous summer fruit, the better in my eyes. There is something quite perverse about turning the best English strawberries into mousses and ice cream. The secret is to match something with the fruit that is a complete complement without being too intense and overpowering. Here, I think, is a classic.

575 ml/18 fl oz full-cream milk

1 vanilla pod, split lengthways

150 g/5 oz caster sugar

5 egg yolks

75 g/2$^{1}/_{2}$ oz plain flour

500 g/1 lb perfectly ripe English strawberries, hulled

1 tsp rose-water

zest of 1 orange

8 small, thin pancakes (see opposite)

double or clotted cream, to serve

1 Place the milk and the vanilla pod together in a pan and bring to the boil.

2 Meanwhile, whisk the sugar and egg yolks together until thick and creamy. Add the flour and whisk to combine. Pour on the boiling milk and stir well.

3 Return the mixture to the pan and cook slowly until the mixture thickens and just – and I mean just – starts to boil. Immediately pour out of the pan into a clean bowl and cover well with cling film to cool.

4 Once completely cool, discard the vanilla pod and gently whisk the pastry cream to let down the mixture, adding the rose-water and orange zest.

5 Fold the strawberries into the pastry cream, taking care not to break up the strawberries too much.

6 Top each of the pancakes with a dollop of pastry cream, then carefully fold over so that you end up with a little envelope. The mixture may be a little runny, so take care when folding.

7 Serve warm or cold, with cream.

Note: These pancakes can be eaten cold, but you can also warm them slightly in a microwave. Warming the pancakes brings out the flavour and perfume of the strawberries. It's best to warm the pancakes in the bowl that you are going to serve them in so that you do not have to move them.

MAKING PANCAKES

The popular myth is that pancakes cannot be stored, but this is not true. They can be made, cooled, then stacked together on top of each other and covered with cling film. They will keep this way in a refrigerator for up to 5 days. They are also very quick to prepare and cook.

Place 2 large egg whites in a deep bowl. Add a pinch of salt, 55 g (2 oz) sieved plain flour and 50 ml (2 fl oz) semi-skimmed milk. Mix well with a whisk to ensure a smooth, lump-free batter. Add another 50 ml (2 fl oz) milk, until you have a thin batter. Take care though not to add too much – if the batter is too thin, the pancakes will be too fragile. Cook in a hot nonstick pan slightly oiled with 1 tablespoon grapeseed or safflower oil until nicely browned on both sides. This recipe will make 4 small pancakes.

Steamed Bananas with Apricot Sauce

Quick and simple, and very tasty, this dessert is excellent served with yoghurt or low-fat crème fraîche.

200 g/7 oz apricots in syrup	2 drops lemon oil
2 ripe bananas, peeled	1 tsp unrefined sugar
1 vanilla pod	low-fat yoghurt or crème fraîche,
4 leaves fresh basil	to serve

1 Place the apricots into a liquidizer or blender, adding enough syrup to blend into a thickish sauce.

2 Lay out 2 large pieces of foil, then place a banana on each one. Fold up the ends of the foil, then spoon the apricot sauce over the bananas. Add the vanilla pod and its seeds, basil leaves and a drop of lemon oil to each one.

3 Fold up the foil into 2 parcels and seal well. Place in a baking tray and pour in 2 cm (³/₄ in) of boiling water. Bring back to the boil on the stove, then place in a preheated oven at 230°C (450°F, Gas mark 8). Cook for 10 minutes, depending on the ripeness of the bananas.

4 Serve the bananas warm, still in their opened parcels, with a large blob of low-fat yoghurt.

The Lunch Box

Ah, the trusty lunch box ... and if you have visions of soggy ham and tomato sandwiches, banish them now. Toting your lunch to work, school or wherever need not be an exercise in drudgery. Getting people to eat – and enjoy – a packed lunch is a simple matter of thinking outside the box, so to speak. Whether it be a wrap, a frittata or a mouthwatering sandwich, the secret is all in using both your imagination and tasty, interesting ingredients.

Orzo Wraps

Bird's tongue pasta, or orzo, as it is known, is a delicious way of getting children to eat pasta. It is easy to eat and easy to wrap in a flour tortilla or one of the numerous breads now available. Pitta bread is a good substitute, as it forms a nice pocket. As for the fillings, I really cannot give that much advice. Every child has different tastes and what works for one child may be an absolute no-no for another. So here is a very simple recipe which appeals to most children ... so far.

175 g/6 oz cooked orzo (bird's tongue pasta)

a little olive oil

100 g/3¹/₂ oz mild Cheddar, finely grated

mayonnaise or salad cream

tin of sweetcorn kernels, well drained

iceberg lettuce, finely chopped

flatbread such as tortilla or pitta

salt and freshly ground black pepper

1 Place the cooked pasta in a large bowl, and pour over a little olive oil to prevent it sticking.

2 Add the Cheddar and enough mayonnaise to bind – do not overdo it.

3 Season lightly, then add some sweetcorn and a little lettuce. Mix well.

4 Spoon into flatbreads and wrap well.

Cucumber and Soft Cheese Wraps

Simple yet interesting, these wraps also make good children's party food or adult picnic food.

4 small wheat tortilla wraps or thin Chinese pancakes

soft cream cheese

$1/2$ cucumber, cut into thin strips as per Chinese-style duck

salad cress or spring onion, very finely shredded

1 tsp Dijon mustard

freshly ground black pepper

1 Spread the cheese onto the wrap nice and thickly. Lay a few cucumber strips and salad cress or spring onion in a strip down the centre. Season with the mustard and plenty of black pepper.

2 Wrap by folding in three of the sides, then rolling the tortilla into a tube. Leave the top end open or slice on the angle into smaller pieces.

SERVES 2   **PREP 20 MINS**   **COOK 20 MINS**

Potato, Herb and Tuna Frittata

I have always enjoyed tinned tuna. It is very versatile and very good for you. My grandma loved the stuff and would eat it with pickled or raw onions. Almost any fish can be used – salmon and fresh dill, prawns and chilli, cod and lentils, and even tinned sardines and pilchards are fine. This is great one-pot food that is cheap and cheerful.

50 g/2 oz unsalted butter

250 g/8 oz potatoes, boiled in their skins, peeled and thinly sliced

½ small onion, very finely chopped

2 x 185 g/6 oz tins tuna, drained

3 large eggs

2 tbsp cold milk

2 tbsp olive oil

2 tbsp freshly chopped oregano

50 g/2 oz mature Cheddar

salt and freshly ground black pepper

1 Heat the butter in a nonstick frying pan until almost sizzling, but do not burn. Add the potato slices, overlapping them slightly. Cook for a few seconds until they colour a little.

2 Sprinkle on the onion and tuna.

3 In a bowl, whisk together the eggs, milk, olive oil and oregano. Season well with salt and pepper.

4 Pour over the potato mixture, sprinkle on the cheese and place under a hot grill or a preheated hot oven (200°C, 400°F, Gas mark 6) for 6–8 minutes until risen and set.

5 Invert the frittata onto a plate and cut into wedges. Serve hot or cold with a blob of mayonnaise. Good supper food and even better picnic food cold, this frittata is also perfect for the lunch box.

Baked Brunch Loaf

The secret with this loaf is that anything can go into it. I have given you a rough example here, but the more flavours and texture you can incorporate, the better. Great lunchbox or picnic food purely because everything you need is in one loaf and easy to transport. I find it's best cooked the day before and chilled well, then eaten at room temperature with a little mayonnaise.

1 large round loaf of bread	4 grilled flat mushrooms
150 g/5 oz black pudding, thinly sliced	115 g/4 oz radicchio, very thinly sliced
3 red peppers, halved and roasted until very soft	8 slices crispy fried streaky bacon
	3 hard-boiled eggs, peeled and sliced
2 large potatoes, thinly sliced and sautéed	salt and freshly ground
6 spring onions, very finely sliced	black pepper
6 thin slices Emmenthal cheese	200 ml/7 fl oz extra virgin olive oil

1 Slice the loaf into horizontally into 4, then brush each slice with a little of the olive oil.

2 Place the black pudding, peppers, potato and spring onion on the base and season well with salt and pepper and a little more olive oil.

3 Next, top with another slice of bread, then with the cheese, mushrooms and radicchio lettuce. Season well.

4 Finally, top with the last slice of bread, bacon and eggs, and again season well.

5 Top with the lid and prick well with a carving fork. Drizzle the olive oil over the top.

6 Wrap in 2 layers of foil and place on a baking sheet, then bake in a preheated oven at 200°C (400°F, Gas mark 6) for 25 minutes.

7 Remove from the oven and press slightly, then chill well.

8 Remove the foil and slice, and serve at room temperature.

SERVES
4

PREP
25
MINS

COOK
15
MINS

Spiced Deep-fried Turkey Filos

Turkey mince is extremely versatile. In fact, not only is it versatile, but it is a very healthy alternative to most meats as well. The only thing you really need to do is add a few spices and bits and pieces to bring out the flavour of the turkey. This recipe is perfect for a spring light lunch or supper dish. The meat remains moist and tender, something that is quite difficult to do. The filos can be made in advance and kept chilled or even frozen, then cooked at the last moment. They are also ideal served cold as a lunch-box or even a picnic dish.

300 g/10 oz turkey mince, free of skin and sinew	1/2 tsp Chinese five-spice powder
	2 tbsp freshly chopped flat-leaf parsley
2 shallots, peeled and finely chopped	1 egg, beaten
3 cloves smoked garlic, peeled and crushed	1 x 270 g/9 oz packet filo pastry
	salt and freshly ground black pepper
1 tbsp freshly chopped green ginger	vegetable oil, for frying

1 Process the turkey, shallots, ginger, garlic, five-spice powder and parsley to a fine paste. Season well with salt and pepper.

2 Place the turkey paste in a bowl. Add half the beaten egg and mix well.

3 Meanwhile, remove the filo pastry from the packet, unroll carefully and keep covered with a clean kitchen cloth until ready to use.

4 Cut the pastry into twelve 33 cm (13 in) strips. Brush a 2 cm (3/4 in) strip down each long side of the pastry strip with beaten egg, then place a spoonful of the turkey mixture in one corner of the top of the filo strip.

Spread into a triangle shape, roughly 5 cm (2 in) across. Spread the turkey mixture out a touch further, then carefully fold the pastry over onto itself, so that the mixture is folded inside the triangle.

5 Repeat the folding process until you end up with a half triangle of pastry left. Brush this completely with the beaten egg and fold over. Seal the edges, gently flatten the filo well to expel any excess air, then place carefully on a tray covered with cling film dusted with a little flour to prevent the triangles sticking. Chill until needed. These parcels will freeze well, if covered with 2 layers of cling film.

6 Heat the vegetable oil in a wok, no more than two-thirds full, until hot. Fry the triangles, 3 at a time, for 3–4 minutes. Flip over and cook the other side for a further 3–4 minutes. Don't do any more than 3 triangles at once, as the heat will decrease rapidly and the filos will not crisp.

7 Transfer to a baking sheet, sprinkle with a little sea salt and black pepper, and keep hot in a warm oven until you have fried all the filos.

8 Drain well on absorbent kitchen paper and serve warm or cold with sweet chilli sauce or lightly pickled peppers.

HINTS AND TIPS

- ► Make sure that all the filo pastry is kept covered while you are not working with it. Otherwise it will dry out extremely quickly.
- ► Do not overcook the turkey, as it will dry out and become very stringy.
- ► You can make this dish using turkey breast escalopes – just remove any fat and skin first as it will not break down successfully in the food processor.
- ► Any spices can be used, although take care not to overpower the delicate flavour of the meat.
- ► The meat basically steams inside the filo coating, keeping it moist. Make sure that the parcels are sealed completely before frying.
- ► Marinating the meat overnight in the spices will increase the flavour of the finished dish enormously.
- ► Chicken, salmon and pork mince are all ideal substitutes for turkey. Experiment for yourself – it's very simple to do.

The Ultimate Layered Sandwich

This really is the ultimate layered sandwich. The secret is to make sure that each layer is liberally drizzled with olive oil and seasoned well. If not, the whole thing will taste bland.

8 slices malted grain bread	1/2 red onion, sliced into fine rings
olive oil	2 small red pickled beetroot
1 red pepper, opened and char-grilled	2 tbsp mayonnaise
1 medium yellow courgette, cut into long slices and char-grilled	2 cooked chicken thighs or drumsticks, meat only
10 marinated anchovies	1 ripe plum tomato, sliced
6 sprigs flat-leaf parsley	a few fresh basil leaves
55 g/2 oz Mozzarella, sliced	salt and freshly ground black pepper

1 Place one slice of bread on a large piece of foil. Season with salt and pepper, and drizzle over 2 tablespoons olive oil. Lay the cooked pepper on top, as flat as possible, and season once again.

2 Top with another slice of bread, season once more, and drizzle over another 2 tablespoons olive oil, then add the courgette.

3 Build up the remaining layers with slices of bread, seasoning and adding another 2 tablespoons oil between each layer. Use the following ingredients together: anchovies and parsley, mozzarella and onions, beetroot and mayonnaise, chicken and, finally, tomato and basil.

4 Top with the last slice of bread and press down fairly hard. Drizzle over a little more olive oil and wrap tightly in the foil. Place on a baking sheet and bake in a preheated oven at 220°C (425°F, Gas mark 7) for 20 minutes.

5 Remove carefully from the oven, press slightly and pack the foil together tightly. Cool, then chill overnight, weighted slightly.

6 Carefully remove the foil. Cut the sandwich into quarters, secure with kebab skewers and arrange on a plate.

7 The colours are fantastic, it really is the best sandwich. You can put whatever you like in the sandwich, just experiment and have fun – it's very difficult to go wrong.

Crab, Ginger and Chilli Wraps

This is one of the tastiest wraps that you can make and eat. The idea for it came from my friend and colleague, Ken Hom, whom I consider the best Chinese chef by a million miles, so thanks, Ken. Fresh crabmeat can be fairly expensive, so look out for the Thai crabmeat in tins. Most of the supermarkets now sell this very good product. Remember that a little crabmeat goes a long way, so it's worth it in the long run.

2 tbsp sunflower oil	2 tsp Thai fish sauce
1 small onion, peeled and finely chopped	1 tbsp red wine vinegar
1 tsp Thai green chilli paste	2 tbsp freshly chopped coriander
1 tsp finely chopped fresh ginger	1 firm ripe avocado, cut into cubes
2 x 240 g/8 oz tins (Thai) crabmeat, well drained	4 large wheat tortillas
	shredded iceberg lettuce
200 g/7 oz mayonnaise	salt and freshly ground black pepper

1 Heat the sunflower oil in a pan, then add the onion, chilli paste and ginger, and cook for 5 minutes to soften. Allow to cool.

2 Place all the ingredients into a bowl apart from the tortillas and lettuce, and season well.

3 Open the tortillas and lay in a little lettuce. Fill generously with the crab mixture and wrap up fairly firmly.

4 Cut each tortilla in half on the angle and serve in a large napkin.

Cold Beef Appetizer

This is a great way to use up all the leftover roast on a Monday or Tuesday. It is so simple and quick, and works equally well with lamb or chicken. All the ingredients are approximate, as this really is 'a make it up as you go along' idea. Just keep tasting and adjusting to your preference, using this recipe as a guideline.

leftover cooked meat (roast is the best for this)	Worcestershire sauce
	Tabasco sauce
2 tbsp hot horseradish sauce	finely chopped onion or shallot
4 tbsp good-quality mayonnaise	freshly chopped thyme

1 Cut the meat into small pieces and mix everything together. Season well.

2 Serve in or with lettuce.

Spiced Sausage and Prune Patties

This combination is a classic and works very well – even my kids eat them. You can vary the fruit you put in. Almost any dried fruit works well with pork, so experiment.

6 ready-to-eat prunes, pitted and finely chopped	2 tsp ground cumin
	2 pinches red chilli powder
450 g/1 lb good-quality sausage meat	1 egg, beaten
2 tbsp freshly chopped sage	salt and freshly ground black pepper
3 tsp ground nutmeg	

1 Mix the prunes with the sausage meat, sage, nutmeg, cumin and chilli powder. Season well with salt and pepper, then if necessary add a little of the beaten egg to bind together. Mould the mixture into 8 patties.

2 Cook the patties over a medium heat on the barbecue for about 15 minutes, turning occasionally, being careful not to let the outsides overcook before the middles are cooked right the way through.

3 Serve warm or cold, with natural yoghurt or salsa dipping sauce.

Marinated Warm Pasta with Cheat's Cherry Tomato Sauce

There is nothing wrong with using a good-quality shop-bought ingredient, then beefing it up with some fresh, interesting ingredients. Here a good base sauce is a great vehicle for a cold pasta salad.

---

500 g/1 lb fresh pappardelle

50 ml/2 fl oz olive oil

1 x 380 g/13 oz good-quality cherry tomato sauce

1 tsp balsamic vinegar

2 tsp freshly chopped basil

2 tsp freshly chopped oregano

1 garlic clove, very finely crushed

4 ripe plum tomatoes cut into small pieces, seeds and all

salt and freshly ground black pepper

---

1 Cook the pasta in a large pan with plenty of boiling water for 3 minutes, or until just tender. Drain through a colander.

2 Transfer the hot pasta to a bowl. Add half the olive oil and mix well, and keep warm.

3 Place the jar of pasta sauce in a separate, large bowl and add the balsamic vinegar, the remaining oil, basil, oregano, garlic and plum tomatoes, and mix well. Season with the salt and pepper.

4 Now add the hot pasta to the sauce. Mix well, cover and leave to cool.

5 Serve cool or just warmed through in a saucepan for a few seconds, with garlic bread and a green salad.

SERVES 4 | **PREP 10 MINS** | **COOK 0 MINS**

Mango and Passionfruit Smoothie

This is not strictly a lunchbox drink, but you could make it up and store it in an insulated flask if you wish. Just give it a good shake before you pour it out. It does, however, make a nice summer breakfast drink packed full of flavour, and is also a delicious drink to serve at an afternoon party.

1 large ripe mango, halved, stone removed and skinned	225 ml/7 fl oz natural yoghurt
2 tbsp caster sugar	juice and pulp of 4 passionfruits, including seeds
900 ml/1½ pints full-cream milk	4 lime wedges

1 Place the ripe mango and sugar into a blender along with the milk and yoghurt. Blitz until smooth.

2 Transfer to a bowl and whisk in the passionfruit juice and pulp.

3 Pour into large glasses and serve decorated with thick wedges of lime.

Family Picnics

Picnics can make for some wonderful memories, particularly when they are family events, and the ideal travelling food can make those memories even better. All it takes is a little planning and you will all be chomping at the bit to dig in to your picnic goodies. The options are endlessly varied – from dips with fresh crusty loaves or flatbread to turnovers and slices of homemade savoury pie. And you don't even have to go without dessert.

Tuscan Bean Dip

This is good picnic food, especially as it can be made up well in advance and actually tastes better if made and left to marinate for a day. Sun blush tomatoes can be replaced by any semi-soft sun-dried tomato and just add whatever herb you want. It's all delicious once marinated. This also makes great party dip food with a large glass of chilled white wine or Champagne.

100 g/3$\frac{1}{2}$ oz cannellini beans	75 g/2$\frac{1}{2}$ oz sun blush tomatoes
100 g/3$\frac{1}{2}$ oz borlotti beans	$\frac{1}{2}$ tsp very finely chopped red chilli
100 g/3$\frac{1}{2}$ oz butter beans	2$\frac{1}{2}$ tbsp virgin olive oil
2 cloves garlic	2$\frac{1}{2}$ tbsp red wine vinegar
1 medium onion, finely chopped	salt and freshly ground black pepper

1 Place the beans, garlic, onion, tomatoes, chilli, olive oil, vinegar and salt and pepper to taste in a food processor. Pulse until you have a rough paste, not too smooth.

2 Turn out into a bowl and add the herbs. Stir well and chill.

3 Serve with pitta breads that have been split in two, drizzled with a little olive oil and baked until crisp.

Smoked Salmon Muffins with Sour Cream, Chives and Beetroot

Smoked salmon and sour cream make a great combination. If you really want to push the boat out, top it with a little real caviar. Or you can buy Avruga caviar, which is herring roe and a snip of the price of the real thing.

115 g/4 oz self-raising flour, sifted	2 tbsp vegetable oil
2 pinches salt	200 g/7 oz smoked salmon, either rolled or finely sliced
freshly ground black pepper	
2 large eggs, separated	150 g/5 oz sour cream
150 ml/5 fl oz cold milk	3 tbsp freshly chopped chives
50 g/2 oz butter, melted	6–8 baby pickled beetroots, sliced
75 g/2^1/$_2$ oz spring onions, finely chopped	caviar (optional)
2 tbsp freshly chopped tarragon	

1 To make the muffins, place the flour, pepper and salt into a large bowl. Add the egg yolks and milk, and mix well.

2 Whip the whites until frothy, but not split. Fold the egg whites into the batter along with the butter, spring onion and tarragon.

3 Heat the oil in 2 individual frying pans or 1 slightly larger pan. Add the batter, making sure that it comes no more than halfway up the sides of the pan, as the mixture will rise. Cook for 2 minutes, then place on the bottom of a preheated grill set at its hottest setting or in a preheated oven at 200°C (400°F, Gas mark 6) to finish cooking. Do not overcook.

4 Meanwhile, mix the sour cream with a little salt and pepper. Add the chives.

5 To serve, turn out the hot muffins onto a plate, then pile on the smoked salmon. Top with the beetroot and spoon over the sour cream. Finally, top with a generous spoon of caviar, if using.

Pasta, Artichoke and Spring Onion Salad

A different way of eating baby tinned artichokes. They are great value for money and have a lot of flavour without the hassle of preparing and cooking them. Tinned or, better still, bottled artichokes are ideal to have on hand in the cupboard. They also make a good quiche.

2 x 400 g/14 oz jars baby artichokes in olive oil	2 tbsp natural yoghurt
15 black olives, pitted and cut in half	2 tbsp mayonnaise
6 spring onions, cut on the slant	1 tbsp sherry vinegar
4 tbsp freshly chopped parsley	225 g/8 oz cooked pasta bows
	salt and freshly ground black pepper

1 Cut each artichoke into 4 wedges. Place in a bowl, add the olives, spring onion and parsley. Mix well.

2 In a separate bowl, mix the yoghurt, mayonnaise, vinegar and salt and pepper to taste.

3 Spoon the yoghurt mixture onto the pasta and mix well. Add the artichoke mixture and stir through, then chill. It's as simple as that.

Baked Corned Beef and Pickle Turnovers

I simply love corned beef hash when it's properly cooked. It's a great winter warmer with loads of potato and onion and topped with my dad's pickled red cabbage. He always used to have great big glass sweet jars filled with the pickle in the garage. However, when I developed some picnic food recipes, I used corned beef with shop-bought pickle instead of the cabbage – it's really tasty.

200 g/7 oz corned beef, chilled overnight and cut into 8 mm ($1/_3$ in) cubes

55 g/2 oz spicy pickle

40 g/$1^1/_2$ oz fresh breadcrumbs

1 tsp freshly chopped thyme

1 egg, beaten, plus extra for egg wash

8 sheets filo pastry, each measuring at least 12 cm x 24 cm/5 in x 10 in

sea salt and freshly ground black pepper

1 Place the corned beef in a bowl. Add the pickle, breadcrumbs, thyme and 1 beaten egg, and season well with pepper.

2 Cut out 16 circles each 12 cm (5 in) in diameter from the filo pastry and cover with a clean kitchen cloth so that the pastry doesn't dry out while you are working with it.

3 Lightly brush one pastry disc with egg wash, then cover with another pastry disc. Lightly brush egg wash over one half of the surface, top with a spoonful of the corned beef mixture, then fold over the other half of the pastry and pinch edges to seal well. Repeat to make more turnovers.

4 Brush the turnovers with egg wash and sprinkle with sea salt, then place on a lightly greased baking sheet. Cook in a preheated oven at 200°C (400°F, Gas mark 6) for about 15 minutes, or until golden. Remove from the oven and allow to cool.

5 Serve with more pickle or pickled onions.

Leek, Sausage and Pickle Pie

My mum used to make a version of this wonderful pie, so I sort of stole the idea from her. We used to eat it with warm new potatoes cooked in a little mint, and a green salad. The best thing about this pie is that it can be transported well, making it ideal for outdoor eating. Two things to remember: make sure that you wash the leeks very well – otherwise it's like eating gritty, sand-filled sandwiches – and use good-quality sausage meat. Cheap sausage meat is full of fat.

1 packet ready-rolled shortcrust pastry sheets	2 tbsp freshly chopped basil
3 medium leeks, split (but still attached at the base), rinsed very well, then bases removed and stalks finely chopped	$^1/_2$ tsp ground black pepper
	a little salt
	1 medium egg
700 g/1$^1/_2$ lb good-quality sausage meat	4 tbsp sweet pickle
	a little beaten egg
	sesame seeds

1 Line a 22 cm x 4 cm (9 in x 1$^3/_4$ in) deep loose-bottomed flan tin with one of the discs of pastry, pushing the pastry well into the base of the tin. Prick the pastry well with a fork, then chill.

2 Bring a large pan of water to the boil, add a little salt and plunge the leeks in. Cook for 3 minutes to soften, then refresh under cold water, drain well and lay on absorbent kitchen paper.

3 Place the sausage meat in a bowl, add the basil, pepper and a little salt. Mix well. Add the egg and mix well again.

4 Place half the sausage meat into the prepared pastry. Lay the leeks on top and season well. Top with the sweet pickle and spread out nice and evenly. Top with the other half of the sausage meat. Pack down well.

5 Moisten the edge of the pastry case with a little beaten egg, lay the other disc of pastry over the top and seal well. Trim off any excess, then crimp the edges.

6 Brush with beaten egg and sprinkle over some sesame seeds, then make 3 incisions in the lid. Bake in a preheated oven at 190°C (375°F, Gas mark 5) for 25–30 minutes, or until light golden in colour.

7 Remove from the oven and leave to cool. Chill well before attempting to cut and eat.

8 Serve cold, accompanied by new potatoes or potato salad.

Andy Knight's Pizza Pane

This recipe is Andy Knight's, a great friend of mine and a pretty good cook. The base remains the same, but you can add all sorts of toppings. The pizzas must be eaten piping hot, straight from the oven, so this is not strictly a picnic recipe unless you are having it in your back garden – and there is nothing wrong with that idea. They are also great as a starter.

For the dough	For the topping
500 g/1 lb strong white bread flour	4 plum tomatoes, chopped into small pieces
75 g /2$^1/_2$ oz fresh yeast, broken up	2 garlic cloves, crushed
1 tbsp caster sugar	small bunch of fresh basil, chopped
1 tbsp salt	100 ml/3$^1/_2$ fl oz extra virgin olive oil
75 ml (2$^1/_2$ fl oz) olive oil, plus a little extra for greasing	salt and freshly ground black pepper
350–400 ml/12–14 fl oz warm water	

1 To make the dough, place the flour, yeast, sugar and salt in a food mixer (with the dough hook attachment fixed if you have one) and set on a low speed. With the mixer operating, gradually add the 75 ml (2$^1/_2$ fl oz) olive oil, then the water, and mix thoroughly – the dough will eventually work itself away from the side of the bowl. Once this stage has been reached, continue to mix for a further 5 minutes.

2 Remove the dough from the mixer and place it in a bowl which has been lightly greased with the extra olive oil. Cover the bowl with cling film and leave the dough to rise in a warm place for about 45 minutes to 1 hour, or until it has doubled in size.

3 Meanwhile, make the topping (or make up your own). Place the tomato in a bowl, then mix in the garlic, basil and oil, and season well. Allow to stand for at least 1 hour to allow the flavours to infuse and develop. (This mixture will keep in a sealed container for up to a week in the refrigerator.)

4 When the dough is ready, preheat the oven to 230°C (450°F, Gas mark 8). Break the dough into 12 pieces, knead each one lightly, then roll out very thinly on a floured surface to approximately 15 cm (6 in) circles. Prick the dough all over with a fork and place on a baking sheet. Spoon on the topping, making sure that the dough bases are not flooded by too much oil. Bake for 10–12 minutes, or until the base is crisp and well risen.

Variations
- Sliced Mozzarella cheese and sun blush tomatoes
- Grated Stilton and chopped walnuts
- Three-bean salad made into a thick purée
- Parmesan cheese with fresh sage and chopped black olives
- Sun-dried tomato paste with grated Pecorino cheese
- Good-quality shop-bought pesto topped with breadcrumbs
- Green olive tapenade with roasted red peppers

Sweet and Spicy Onion Dip

This dip I picked up when I was in the United States about three years ago, so I cannot take the credit for it. The lady's name was Diane Dodge, and I went to a birthday party at her very nice woodland home. The highlight of the party was her onion dip. In the United States, they have vidalia onions that are very sweet – some people say that you can eat them like an apple. This I have yet to try, but I have no reason to disbelieve, as the dip was sweet, melting and delicious.

50 g/2 oz unsalted butter	1 tsp Tabasco sauce
3 medium onions, peeled and finely chopped	1 tbsp Worcestershire sauce
2 cloves garlic, crushed	1 tsp caster sugar
225 g/8 oz strong Cheddar, grated	3 tbsp smoked sweet paprika
225 g/8 oz good-quality mayonnaise	salt and freshly ground black pepper

1 Heat the butter in a pan, add the onion and garlic, and cook for about 15 minutes to soften.

2 Remove the pan from the heat and stir in the Cheddar, mayonnaise, Tabasco, Worcestershire sauce, sugar and, finally, a good seasoning of salt and pepper.

3 Put the mixture into a ceramic baking dish, sprinkle evenly with the paprikaand cook in a preheated oven at 200°C (400°F, Gas mark 6) for 20 minutes. Remove and allow to cool slightly.

4 Eat warm, with plenty of bread sticks, crackers or Melba toast.

Stuffed Vine Leaves

One of my favourites, when cooked properly, stuffed vine leaves, or dolmades, are delicious. I have added a twist of my own with a little garlic and saffron. Beginning with half-cooked rice makes it easier to roll up the leaves.

90 ml/3 fl oz olive oil, plus extra for drizzling

1 small onion, finely chopped

1 clove garlic, crushed

1/2 tsp ground cumin

225 g/8 oz long-grain rice, half cooked and refreshed

3 tbsp freshly chopped dill

3 tbsp freshly chopped mint

vine leaves, soaked in boiling water

pinch of saffron threads

600 ml/1 pint strong vegetable stock, boiling

3–4 tbsp freshly squeezed lemon juice

salt and freshly ground black pepper

1 Heat the 90 ml (3 fl oz) olive oil in a small pan and add the onion, garlic and cumin, and cook for 3 minutes.

2 Transfer to a bowl and add the rice. Mix well before adding the dill and mint. Season well with the salt and pepper, and stir through again.

3 Place one vine leaf on a flat surface and put a spoonful of the rice mixture into the middle of the leaf. Fold up carefully and repeat until all the mixture is used up. Pack the stuffed vine leaves fairly tightly into a shallow pan – make sure that it's ovenproof.

4 Add the saffron to the boiling stock and infuse. Pour over the stuffed vine leaves – *just* cover the vine leaves. Add the lemon juice.

5 Place the pan on the stove and bring to a gentle simmer, then place a plate on top of the stuffed vine leaves and cover with the lid. Pop into a preheated oven at 200°C (400°F, Gas mark 6) and cook for 35 minutes, or until the vine leaves are plump and full. All the stock should be absorbed.

6 Lightly drizzle a little olive oil over the vine leaves and leave to cool before eating. A nice bowl of tzatziki is perfect with these.

SERVES	PREP	PICKLE	COOK
4	30 MINS	24 HOURS	10 MINS

Sweet Pickled Prawns with Lime and Coriander Mayonnaise

This is an idea I picked up while travelling in the United States. The sweet pickle is a nice twist and works well with the lime and coriander mayonnaise.

200 ml/7 fl oz malt vinegar

2 heaped tbsp caster sugar

4 tbsp olive oil

1 tbsp crushed fennel seed

pinch of red chilli powder

3 bay leaves

2 shallots, very finely chopped

juice of 2 fresh limes

2 tbsp freshly chopped dill

1/2 tsp dried mustard powder

4 tbsp vegetable oil

20 large, raw freshwater prawns, heads removed, peeled and deveined, with tail shell left intact

salt and freshly ground black pepper

Lime and Coriander Mayonnaise

225 g/8 oz good-quality mayonnaise

2 cloves garlic, crushed

juice of 1 lime

1 tbsp Worcestershire sauce

2 tbsp sweet chilli sauce

1 Place the vinegar, sugar, olive oil, fennel seed, chilli powder, bay leaves and shallots into a stainless steel saucepan. Season with a little salt and pepper, and bring to the boil. Simmer for 3 minutes, so the shallot softens, then remove from the stove and cool completely.

2 Taste the cooled marinade and adjust the seasoning if necessary, then add the lime juice, dill and dried mustard powder. Mix well with a whisk.

3 Place the vegetable oil into a wok and heat until just smoking. Add the prawns in 2 batches. Season well and cook until they turn a bright pink, but do not overcook.

4 Strain in a colander, then carefully lay the prawns in a flat glass, ceramic or stainless steel tray or dish, so that they are two deep.

5 Pour the marinade over the prawns, cover and leave to marinate for 12 hours or overnight in the refrigerator, turning a couple of times.

6 Mix the mayonnaise with the coriander, garlic, lime juice, Worcestershire sauce and sweet chilli sauce. Season well with salt and pepper.

7 To serve, first drain the prawns well. Spoon the mayonnaise onto a piece of crusty bread and top with a prawn or two. Delicious.

SERVES	PREP	MARINATE	COOK
4	15 MINS	2 HOURS	0 MINS

Marinated Peaches with Lime and Mascarpone

The secret here is to make sure the peaches you choose are really ripe. I normally allow one and a half peaches per person.

6 ripe peaches or nectarines, sliced into wedges

unrefined icing sugar, to taste

2–3 tbsp peach liqueur

juice of 1 lime

4–5 tbsp shredded fresh mint or lemon verbena

Vanilla Mascarpone Cream

250 g/8 oz mascarpone cheese

icing sugar, to taste

1 vanilla pod, split lengthways

a little milk (optional)

1 Lay the peaches on a ceramic or glass tray or bowl. Sprinkle over the unrefined icing sugar, then drizzle over the peach liqueur and lime juice. Finally, sprinkle over the mint. Cover and leave to marinate for at least 2 hours.

2 To make the mascarpone cream, beat the mascarpone with just enough icing sugar to taste – do not use too much, as it must not be too sweet.

3 Carefully scrape the seeds out of the vanilla pod and add to the mascarpone. Mix well. (You may want to add a touch of milk to make the end result a little lighter.)

4 Spoon the peaches into individual dishes and serve with the vanilla mascarpone cream.

Lemon Cheesecake

This can be a tricky recipe, so take care. The secret is to finish the cheesecake mixture before it sets too much to pour into the prepared flan base.

1 x pkt digestive biscuits, crushed (about 20 biscuits)	3 egg whites
butter, melted	pinch of cream of tartar
350 g/12 oz cream cheese, at room temperature	3^1/$_2$ leaves gelatine, soaked in plenty of water
175 g/6 oz caster sugar, plus 50 g/2 oz extra	grated zest and juice of 2 large lemons
	275 ml/9 fl oz whipping cream, very lightly whipped

1 Mix the biscuits and melted butter together – use just enough butter so that the crumbs are coated, but not so much that they become soggy. Line a greased 23 cm x 3 cm (11 in x 1^1/$_4$ in) flan base with removable bottom with the biscuit mixture to form a base. Chill well.

2 Place the cream cheese and the 175 g (6 oz) caster sugar in a mixing bowl and beat on a high speed until thick and creamy.

3 Whip the egg whites with the cream of tartar until foamy but not split. Add the extra caster sugar and continue to beat until soft peaks form.

4 Lift the gelatine out of the water and place in a pan. Add the lemon juice and zest, bring to just under the boil and dissolve the gelatine. Leave to cool for 2 minutes.

5 Pour the gelatine and lemon juice over the cream cheese mixture and whisk well. Remove from the machine, quickly fold in the cream, then the egg whites. Take care at this point, as the mixture may start to set. You need to work quickly. Pour into the chilled base and chill well.

6 Serve accompanied by ice cream or double cream.

SERVES 6–8

PREP 10 MINS

COOK 0 MINS

Chilled Fresh Strawberry Cordial

A really nice way to use up over-ripe strawberries. The fresh taste is amazing.

450 g/1lb fresh over-ripe strawberries	600 ml/1 pint water
225 g/8 oz soft brown sugar	lime or lemon slices
juice of 1/2 lime	ice cubes

1 Mash the soft strawberries with the brown sugar and lime juice (I find a potato masher is best for this) and allow to stand for 1 hour at room temperature to marinate, stirring occasionally.

2 Add the water to the strawberries and stir well, then taste to check the flavour – if it's too sweet, add a little more water. Fold a damp clean kitchen towel in half and use to line a colander or large sieve, pour in the strawberry water and cover the whole thing with cling film. Let stand in a refrigerator overnight – during this time most of the juice will strain through.

3 Next morning, carefully gather up the four corners of the tea towel and gently squeeze out any remaining juice – do not squeeze too much or the liquid will be cloudy.

4 You will be left with a beautiful clear, perfumed strawberry water. Adjust the taste with a little more lime juice if you want to and serve in small tumblers with a slice of fresh lime or lemon and plenty of ice.

Superfast Weekday Suppers

If you dread hearing the words 'What's for supper?' take heart. Actually, banish the thought from your mind completely. You really don't need a huge gap in your busy timetable to produce a plateful of tasty, nutritious food to tempt the fussiest of eaters. In fact, the recipes in this chapter are superquick to prepare and super-easy to plan for, even allowing for a hectic schedule – although you may be a little dismayed at how superfast they are eaten!

Club Sandwich

This is my favourite sandwich. My good friend Richard Delany, an American, makes the best, so here is his recipe.

2 chicken breasts	12 slices of bread, crusts on
2 tbsp olive oil	1/4 iceberg lettuce, very finely chopped
a few sprigs of rosemary, bruised	4 tbsp good-quality mayonnaise
8 rashers dry-cured bacon	8 ripe baby plum tomatoes, thinly sliced
2 tbsp maple syrup	salt and freshly ground black pepper

1 Cut the chicken breasts open, season well with salt and pepper, drizzle over the olive oil and bruised rosemary and leave to marinate for 20 minutes.

2 Heat the grill and lay the bacon out on the grill pan. Drizzle over the maple syrup and gently grill the bacon until nice and crispy, but not burnt. Keep warm while you grill or fry the chicken for 10 minutes on each side until cooked.

3 Toast the bread and keep warm.

4 Mix the lettuce and mayonnaise together.

5 Lay a piece of toast on a chopping board, spoon on a little lettuce and mayonnaise, then top with 2 rashers of bacon and a few tomato slices. Lay on the next slice of toast, a little more lettuce, sliced chicken and a few more slices of tomato. Place the last slice of toast on top. Make sure that you season each layer with plenty of salt and pepper.

6 Cut into triangles and skewer with frilly cocktail sticks. Serve immediately. The only thing to drink with these delicious sandwiches is a very cold beer.

Hot Mushroom Salad

A very simple fragrant salad which makes a great starter or main course. The secret is to have *very* dry mushrooms, and only cook half of them at a time. This ensures that the wok remains hot and the mushrooms fry, rather than boil (they are 90 per cent water).

2 cloves garlic, peeled	2 shallots, finely sliced
90 ml/3 fl oz olive oil	1/2 tsp very finely chopped fresh red chilli
100 g/3 1/2 oz shiitake mushrooms	salad leaves, including frisée, watercress,
100 g/3 1/2 oz wood blewit mushrooms	iceberg lettuce and rocket
100 g/3 1/2 oz grey oyster mushrooms	croûtons
100 g/3 1/2 oz flat mushrooms	salt and freshly ground black pepper

1 The day before, slightly crush the garlic and add to the olive oil to infuse.

2 The next day, pick over the mushrooms and wash if necessary. If you do wash them, make sure that you dry them well – the best thing for this is a salad spinner. This will ensure that they are very dry for frying.

3 Heat a wok or large frying pan and add half the garlic-infused oil, then heat until very hot. Add half the mushrooms and cook for 2–3 minutes, stirring all the time. Add half the shallots and chilli, and stir well. Season well with salt and pepper and stir well, do not overcook the mushrooms.

4 Tip the first batch of cooked mushrooms into a bowl and keep warm while you cook the rest with the remaining oil, shallots and chilli as above.

5 Have a large bowl ready with a selection of salad leaves, then add all of the hot mushrooms and quickly mix well.

6 Adjust the seasoning and pile the salad onto large plates, then top with the croutons. Eat straight away.

CROUTONS
To make croutons, remove the crusts from 2 thick slices of bread, then cut the bread into small cubes. Pan-fry in a little butter and olive oil until golden and crisp. Drain on absorbent kitchen paper.

Salmon with Rice Pancakes and Five-Minute Leeks

A friend of mine once showed me this method of cooking salmon. Dear Ken Hom was cooking this sort of food when I was in short pants. He still is the best Chinese cook on television anywhere. This dish is very simple to produce and delicious to eat. The accompanying leeks truly do only take 5 minutes to cook, and this really the best way to cook them, the only exception being in cheese sauce with smoky bacon.

4 dried rice flour pancakes

4 salmon fillets, about 115 g/4 oz each

sprinkle of lemon grass powder

4 sprigs fresh tarragon

2 tbsp vegetable oil

1 glass fruity white wine (Vigonier is perfect)

3 tbsp good-quality Chinese oyster sauce

1/2 tsp chopped fresh red chilli

1 tsp caster sugar

a little cornflour and water, mixed together to make a paste

salt and freshly ground black pepper

Five-Minute Leeks

2 medium leeks, with a little of the green stalk left on

50 g/2 oz unsalted butter

2 tbsp olive oil

salt and freshly ground black pepper

1 Soak the rice pancakes in cold water until flaccid and soft. Drain well in a clean tea towel and pat dry.

2 Season the salmon fillets well and sprinkle with a little lemon grass powder. Top with a sprig of tarragon.

3 Lay one of the pancakes out on a chopping board and place one of the salmon fillets on top so that the tarragon is now underneath the fillet. Season the top of the fillet.

4 Fold the edges of the pancake onto the salmon fillet. Turn the entire parcel over and rest the folds underneath. You will now be able to see the tarragon through the rice pancake. Repeat the process with the remaining 3 pancakes.

5 Heat the vegetable oil in a nonstick frying pan until quite hot. Add the pancakes fold-side down and cook for 5 minutes, then turn over and cook for a further 5 minutes on the other side. Remove from the pan and drain on absorbent kitchen paper.

6 To make the sauce, place the white wine, oyster sauce and chilli in a pan. Bring to the boil and simmer for a minute or so. Add the sugar and thicken slightly with the cornflour paste. Leave fairly light – you do not want it to thicken too much.

7 To serve, place a spoonful of leeks on each warm plate, top with the salmon parcels and drizzle over a little of the wine sauce.

FIVE-MINUTE LEEKS
1 Slice the leek from top to bottom, leaving the whole thing attached at the root end. Turn the leek and make the same incision, so that you end up with 4 pieces attached at the root end. Wash well, then slice as thinly as possible. Drain thoroughly.

2 Heat the butter and oil together, until the bubbling subsides, then add the leeks and stir well. Season with a little salt and pepper, and cook until the leeks just start to soften. Spoon into a colander, reserving the buttery juices.

3 To serve, warm in a little of the strained reserved juices.

Quick Chicken Stew

This really does cook in 20 minutes and is a great standby if you have to knock something up quickly.

25 g/1 oz butter	285 ml/9^1/$_2$ fl oz fresh chicken stock
1 large leek, sliced and rinsed well	200 ml/7 fl oz double cream
1 red onion, finely sliced	1 tsp wholegrain mustard
4 chicken breast fillets, about 150 g/5 oz each, all skin and bone removed, cut into 2.5 cm/1 in cubes	1^1/$_2$ tbsp freshly chopped tarragon
	squeeze of lemon juice
	salt and freshly ground black pepper
125 ml/4 fl oz dry white wine	boiled new potatoes, to serve

1 Heat the butter in a pan, add the leek and onion, and cook gently until softened. Remove the vegetables from the pan using a slotted spoon and keep warm on a plate.

2 Add the chicken to the same pan and cook quickly to brown all over. Pour the wine and stock into the pan with the chicken and bring to the boil, then reduce the heat and simmer for about 10 minutes, or until the chicken is cooked through.

3 Return the leek and onion to the pan with the cream, mustard and tarragon. Stir and season with salt and pepper, then simmer for a further 5 minutes.

4 Add the squeeze of lemon juice to taste, spoon the stew into bowls and serve with boiled new potatoes.

SERVES	PREP	COOK
6	20 MINS	25 MINS

Moroccan Lamb Patties

Very popular in Morocco, these meat patties are almost treated as a snack. The hardest part is getting all the shopping, but from then on it's all down hill.

2 tbsp vegetable oil	finely grated zest of 1/2 lemon
2 cloves garlic	4 slices dry bread, made into fresh
1 small onion, finely chopped	breadcrumbs
250 g/8 oz very lean lamb mince	1 x 270 g/9 oz packet filo pastry
1 tsp ground cinnamon	beaten egg
1 heaped tsp ground cumin	oil for frying
pinch of chilli powder	salt and freshly ground black pepper
125 ml /4 fl oz lamb or chicken stock	
2 tbsp freshly chopped parsley	**To Serve**
2 tbsp freshly chopped mint	thick natural yoghurt
3 tbsp freshly chopped coriander	freshly chopped mint leaves

1 Heat the vegetable oil in a small frying pan over a low heat. Add the garlic and onion, and cook until softened.

2 Add the lamb, cinnamon, cumin, chilli powder, salt and pepper to taste and stock, and cook for 15 minutes. Remove from the heat, add the parsley, mint, coriander and lemon zest, and leave to cool.

3 Once cooled, add enough breadcrumbs to make a stiff mixture, then adjust the seasoning.

4 Cut the filo pastry into rectangular strips about 10 cm/4 in wide. Cover with a damp cloth so that the pastry doesn't dry out. Spoon a little of the lamb mixture along one long side of the filo pastry, fold over the ends and roll up, sealing all the meat inside. Lightly brush a little egg over the end to seal. Repeat until all the lamb mixture has been used.

5 Shallow-fry in hot oil until crispy and golden. Drain well on absorbent kitchen paper.

6 Serve hot, with thick yoghurt and mint for dipping.

Bubble and Squeak with Poached Egg and Butter Sauce

Most people put cabbage in their bubble and squeak, but Brussels sprouts are the best by far. This very quick butter sauce is ideal for the potatoes and kale. Great telly food – even Fern's kids tuck into the bubble and squeak, but I think we still have a little way to go with the kale.

500 g/1 lb cold mashed potato, no milk or butter

1 leek, trimmed, rinsed well, chopped and cooked in a little butter or oil

about 10 medium Brussels sprouts, well cooked and chopped

1 egg yolk

white wine vinegar

2–3 tbsp vegetable oil

plain flour for dusting

200 g/7 oz curly kale, stalks removed, cooked in boiling salted water until soft, then refreshed

a little butter

4 large eggs

salt and freshly ground black pepper

Quick and Easy Butter Sauce

2 tbsp white wine vinegar

1/2 glass dry white wine

pinch of salt

freshly ground black pepper

2 tbsp whipping cream

60 g/2 oz cold butter, cubed

1 Mix the potato, Brussels sprouts, leek and egg yolk together well. Season with salt and pepper to taste – the mixture should be quite dry and firm.

2 Mould the potato mixture into 4 cakes. Do not make them too thin or it will be difficult to turn them over when cooking.

3 To make the butter sauce, put the vinegar, white wine, salt and pepper to taste into a saucepan and bring to the boil. Reduce the liquid until you have 2–3 tablespoons left. Pop in the cream and bring back to the boil. Cook until the sauce starts to thicken. Remove from the heat and add the butter in small cubes, whisking all the time. The sauce will thicken naturally. Check the seasoning and adjust if needed. Keep warm and covered until needed. (Remember that this sauce is almost like a seasoning, so you only need a small amount.)

4 Place a saucepan of cold water on the stove and season well with salt and white wine vinegar. Bring to the boil.

5 Meanwhile, heat the vegetable oil in a frying pan. Dust the potato cakes with flour on both sides. Carefully add to the pan and cook nice and slowly until golden, then flip over with a fish slice or palette knife. Cook for a further 5–6 minutes. Keep warm.

6 Finally, once the water is on a rolling boil, pop in 2 of the eggs and reduce the heat. Poach until the eggs are cooked, remove and repeat with the other 2 eggs.

7 Warm the kale in a little salt and pepper and butter. Place the potato cakes in the centre of a large plate, spoon on a little kale, top with a poached egg and drizzle over a little of the butter sauce.

SERVES 4-6   **PREP 20 MINS**   **COOK 40 MINS**

Jubby Pie

This seems to work very well with children, probably because they cannot see the inside! The principle remains the same: plenty of potato and thin layers of finely puréed fillings. Stick to pale greens rather than deep greens – i.e. the inside of the cabbage, the middle part of a leek – if do not want to startle the kids.

2 tbsp vegetable oil	2 tbsp flour
1 medium onion, finely chopped	6 tbsp tomato ketchup
1 medium leek, pale green part only, sliced	150 ml/5 fl oz chicken stock, boiling
200 g/7 oz turkey or chicken mince, no skin or fat	salt and freshly ground black pepper
50 g/2 oz frozen peas	750 g/1½ lb warm mashed potatoes, with butter and milk added, but not too loose
1 small carrot, finely chopped	unsalted butter, melted
1 stick celery, finely chopped	grated cheese (optional)

1 Heat the vegetable oil in a pan until sizzling. Add the onion and leek, and cook for 5 minutes to soften.

2 Add the turkey, peas, carrot and celery, and cook for a further 10 minutes.

3 Next add the flour and ketchup, and mix well, then add the boiling stock and bring to the boil, stirring all the time. Cook for 10 minutes, or until the vegetables are cooked. Place the whole lot into a food processor and blitz until smooth. Spoon into a bowl.

4 Place a layer of mashed potato in the bottom of an ovenproof dish. Top with the puréed mixture. Repeat until the dish is full, finishing with a topping of potato.

5 Cover the top of the potato well with the melted butter and cook in a preheated oven at 220°C (435°F, Gas mark 7) for 25 minutes until the top is nicely browned and crunchy. If the kids like cheese, then top with the cheese before glazing.

6 Serve hot with green peas or sweetcorn. This dish can also be made in batches and freezes perfectly – just defrost and reheat in a moderate oven.

Quick Asparagus and Pasta Stir-Fry with Yellow Bean Sauce

Some bottled sauces are excellent and Chinese yellow bean is a cracker. Asparagus works very well with yellow bean. Just add a touch of pasta and, hey presto, a full meal. Only use young asparagus for this dish, as it has to cook in 2–3 minutes.

450 g/1 lb young English asparagus, cut into 3 cm/1¼ in pieces	1 small onion, very finely chopped
3 tbsp vegetable oil	300 g/10 oz rigatoni pasta, cooked
1 tbsp very finely chopped fresh ginger	4 tbsp Chinese yellow bean sauce
	salt and freshly ground black pepper

1 Blanch the asparagus in boiling water for 15 seconds, then refresh in fresh cold water. Set aside.

2 Heat the vegetable oil in a wok over a high heat and add the ginger, then cook for 30 seconds.

3 Add the onion and cook for a further minute to brown.

4 Next, add the asparagus and cook for another minute.

5 Finally, add the cooked pasta, salt and pepper to taste and yellow bean sauce, and stir well.

6 Serve with boiled rice.

Marinated Lamb Chops with Mint, Thyme and Seed Mustard

Lamb chops are Fern's favourite supper dish above all else, so I cook this quite often. Like most of my food, this is a very simple idea, but the sweetness of the mint jelly and the sharpness of the mustard and zest work perfectly with the meat. The best thing to do is to make up the marinade and leave the whole lot for 24 hours. The only thing to serve with this is dauphinoise potatoes.

4 tbsp mint jelly	**Dauphinoise Potatoes**
4 tsp freshly chopped thyme	600 ml/1 pint whipping cream
2 tbsp wholegrain mustard	2 garlic cloves, crushed
finely grated zest of 1 lemon	800 g (1³/₄ lb) potatoes, peeled and
12 lamb loin chops or cutlets, as lean as	thinly sliced lengthways*
possible, trimmed of any excess fat	55 g/2 oz Gruyère cheese,
2 tbsp olive oil	grated (optional)
salt and freshly ground black pepper	salt and freshly ground black pepper

1 Mix together the mint jelly, thyme, mustard and zest, and spread over both sides of the chops. Place on a non-metallic plate or dish, and cover and leave to marinate in the refrigerator overnight – or longer if you have time.

2 To make the dauphinoise potatoes, pour the cream into a pan, add the garlic and bring to the boil. Season the potatoes all over and lay in a shallow ovenproof dish of about 2–2.5 litre (3½–4½ pint) capacity. Pour over the cream mixture and cook in a preheated oven at 200°C (400°F, Gas mark 6) for 25–30 minutes, or until tender.

3 Meanwhile, drizzle the olive oil over the chops and season well with salt and pepper. Cook under a preheated medium grill for 5–7 minutes on each side until cooked to taste. The fat should crisp up nicely, but do take care, as the sugar in the jelly can catch and burn quite quickly. If you prefer, you can cook the chops in a griddle or frying pan.

4 If using, sprinkle the Gruyère cheese over the top of the potatoes and return to the oven until just melting. Serve the lamb with the bubbling pot of dauphinoise potatoes.

* If you have one, a Japanese mandolin is perfect for this job, but mind your fingers!

Potato, Cheddar and Red Onion Chowder with Bacon and Parsley

I like chunky soups and this recipe is so easy and quick. It's very similar to a broth and is packed with flavour. Why not experiment with different ingredients and make up your own chowder? Just remember that tastiness is the key.

2 tbsp vegetable oil	3 rashers back bacon, cut into large pieces
2 small red onions, chopped	300 ml (1/2 pint) milk
1 garlic clove, crushed	2 tbsp freshly chopped parsley
55 g/2 oz plain flour	350 g/12 oz mature Cheddar, cut into small chunks
850 ml (1 1/2 pints) vegetable stock, boiling	
3 medium potatoes, peeled and cut into large chunks	salt and freshly ground black pepper
	crusty bread, to serve

1 Heat the vegetable oil in an ovenproof casserole dish. Add the onion and garlic, and cook gently for a few minutes until soft but not coloured.

2 Add the flour and stir in well until it is absorbed, then gradually add the stock, stirring continuously to prevent lumps forming.

3 Next add the potato and bacon, and season well. Cover with a lid and cook in a preheated oven at 150°C (300°F, Gas mark 2) for 25–30 minutes, or until the potatoes are tender.

4 Remove the cooked chowder from the oven and stir in the milk and parsley to give a nice, thick chowder.

5 Just before serving, stir in the Cheddar, then pour into deep bowls and serve with fresh crusty bread.

HINTS AND TIPS
- ▶ Sweetcorn and mussels are also a great combination in a chowder.
- ▶ This dish will not burn on the bottom of the dish because it is cooked in the oven, rather than on the hob.
- ▶ You can replace the Cheddar with your favourite cheese – they're all great in chowders.
- ▶ The soup can be cooked, cooled and kept in the refrigerator for 3–4 days without spoiling.

Prawn and Avocado Tortilla Sandwich with Pickled Red Onion

On a recent trip to New York, I had a version of this sandwich and simply had to come home and make one very similar. The variations are enormous, but keep to the basics: avocado, coriander, lime and garlic. Pastrami works well, as does smoked chicken – it's really up to you.

2 tbsp vegetable oil

12 freshwater prawns, peeled and deveined, cut into $\frac{1}{2}$ cm/$\frac{1}{4}$ in pieces

2 tsp ground cumin

2 cloves garlic, chopped

juice of 1 lime

1 medium corn on the cob, kernels sliced off and cooked in a hot wok until coloured slightly

1 ripe avocado, roughly mashed with a fork

4 tbsp freshly chopped coriander

175 g/6 oz Cheddar, finely grated

6 x 18 cm/7 in fresh soft tortillas

3 tbsp olive oil

salt and freshly ground black pepper

Picked Red Onion

2 small red onions, peeled and sliced into very thin rings

125 ml/4 fl oz white wine vinegar

juice of 4 large limes

2 tsp sugar

salt and freshly ground black pepper

1 To make the pickled red onion, place the onion, vinegar, lime juice, sugar and salt and pepper to taste into a bowl. Stir through and leave to marinate for 1 hour.

2 Heat the vegetable oil in a wok, add the prawns and cook for 3 minutes, or until cooked.

3 Next, add the cumin and garlic, and cook for a further minute. Finally, add the lime juice and remove the wok from the heat. Spoon the prawns into a bowl.

4 Add the corn, avocado, coriander and Cheddar. Season well with salt and pepper, and mix through.

5 To assemble the sandwich, lay 2 tortillas onto a baking sheet, top each with a little prawn mixture, cover each one with another tortilla and top again with the filling. Finally, top with the last 2 tortillas.

6 Drizzle over the olive oil and place under a preheated hot grill for 3–4 minutes until slightly crispy. Make sure that the grill is not too hot – otherwise the tortillas will burn.

7 To serve, cut into wedges and top with the pickled red onion.

Cooking the Perfect Steak

For me, the only two ways to cook steak are to pan-fry or grill on a barbecue. I would forget grilling, the reason being that most grills do not have enough heat and are too inconsistent in heat spread. Cooking steaks is very easy to get right, but also very easy to get wrong.

PAN-FRYING

The best way to pan-fry a 225 g (8 oz) steak is to place 2–3 tablespoons vegetable oil into a frying pan and heat. Add a small knob of unsalted butter and heat also until it just starts to change colour. Season the steak well with salt and black pepper, and place in the hot butter and oil. Cook over a fairly high heat for 4–5 minutes until nicely coloured.

Turn over and repeat on the other side, turn the heat off and leave the steak to rest for 2 minutes before turning once again. This will ensure a nice medium-rare, juicy steak with plenty of flavour. Just cook for 2–3 minutes longer on each side for a more well-done steak.

Remember, steak is only tough if it has not been hung long enough, so ask your butcher for the hanging times. A good rule of thumb is between 15 and 20 days.

BARBECUING

Barbecue steak has a smoky flavour second to none. Just ensure that you light the barbecue well in advance and leave the coals to turn to a light grey colour before you start to cook. I like to bank up one end of the barbecue, so you then have a cooking area with a spread from cool to hot.

The best tip I can give when cooking on a barbecue is to use a pastry brush or something similar to rub a little vegetable oil over the steaks. Then season with salt and black pepper. This will stop what they call 'flare up' when any excess oil runs off and ignites. Not only does this cause the steak to look burnt, but the horrid black flames lick around the steak and make it taste rancid. So do take care.

Classic Steak Garnishes

Here are four great steak garnishes, any one of which is the ideal complement to the perfect steak. The first is a classic French butter from my apprenticeship. Onion rings are the only thing to have with steak apart from chips. Use any of them to accompany steak whenever you have a particular hankering for them.

Café de Paris Butter

225 g/7 oz unsalted butter, softened	1 tbsp brandy
touch of tomato ketchup	1/2 tsp paprika
1/2 tsp English mustard	dash of Worcestershire sauce
2 shallots, very finely chopped	pinch of curry powder
2 tbsp freshly chopped parsley	finely grated zest and juice of 1 lemon
2 tbsp freshly chopped tarragon	salt and freshly ground
1 clove garlic, crushed	black pepper

1 Simply mix all the ingredients together thoroughly and roll in cling film. Chill well.

2 To use, remove the cling film, cut into slices and top the cooked steak.

The Best Onion Rings

plain flour	milk
freshly chopped parsley	salt and freshly ground
1 large onion, peeled and cut into rings	black pepper
1/2 cm/1/4 in thick	

1 Just place flour into two bowls and add the chopped parsley to one of the bowls, about 4 tbsp to 225 g (8 oz) flour. Season both bowls of flour well.

2 Pour the milk into another bowl, then dip the onion rings first into the plain flour, then the milk and finally into the parsleyed flour, taking care to coat evenly. Deep-fry in very hot oil (185°C, 350°F) until crisp and golden.

3 Drain well on absorbent kitchen paper and season with salt. Serve hot.

Béarnaise Sauce

10 crushed black peppercorns	a little lemon juice
50 ml/2 fl oz tarragon vinegar	4 x 6 cm (2 in) sprigs fresh tarragon,
50 ml/2 fl oz dry white wine	chopped
4 egg yolks	salt and freshly ground
175 g/6 oz unsalted butter, melted	black pepper

1 Place the peppercorns, tarragon vinegar and white wine into a pan and reduce in volume by half.

2 Place the egg yolks and hot vinegar reduction into a bowl and whisk over a pan of simmering water. Cook until frothy and thick.

3 Remove from the heat and gradually beat in the melted butter until totally homogenized.

4 Season well with salt and pepper and a little lemon juice.

5 Finally fold in the chopped tarragon and use straight away if possible. This sauce should only be kept warm for about 15 minutes before using.

Quick Brandy, Peppercorn and Mustard Cream

15 g/1/2 oz unsalted butter	275 ml/9 fl oz well-flavoured
2 tsp crushed black peppercorns	beef stock
2 shallots, very finely chopped	175 ml/6 fl oz double cream
3–4 tbsp brandy	salt
2 tbsp French mustard	squeeze of lemon juice

1 Place the butter, peppercorns and shallots in a small pan and cook over a low heat to soften, about 2 minutes.

2 Add the brandy and flame, stir in the mustard and beef stock, and reduce in volume by about half.

3 Add the cream and bring to the boil. Remove from the heat, season to taste with salt and add the lemon juice. Keep warm until needed.

Baked Apples with Toffee and Pecan Ice Cream

This one of the easiest puds I know. You can make the ice cream if you want to, but there is a huge amount of good-quality ice creams now on the market. For this dessert to work, you really need good old-fashioned Bramleys. They are the best ones to cook quickly and semi-soufflé at the same time. Eat this pudding warm not hot. Otherwise the apple 'marmalade' (the cooked inside of the apple) will burn your mouth.

2 medium Bramley apples, halved horizontally and cored*	2 tbsp soft brown sugar
	toffee pecan ice cream, to serve
55 g/2 oz unsalted butter	maple syrup

1 Place the butter in a nonstick frying pan (suitable for use in the oven) and heat until just starting to brown. Add the sugar and stir well.

2 Put the apples cut-side down in the buttery mixture and heat through. Transfer the contents of the pan to an ovenproof dish and place in a preheated oven at 220°C (425°F, Gas mark 7).

3 Cook for about 10 minutes, then remove from the oven, flip the apples over and return to the oven. Spoon over some of the sugary butter and cook for a further 5–10 minutes, depending on the oven. You want to end up with the apples cooked and slightly souffléed, but not falling to pieces. When soft, remove from the oven and leave to cool for about 10 minutes.

4 To serve, place on plates and fill the apple centres with a ball of pecan ice cream, then drizzle over a little maple syrup.

* Use a scoop or teaspoon to remove the apple cores, leaving a small hole. Take care not to remove too much, or the apples will collapse when cooked.

Fresh Pineapple with Crème de Cacao and Caramel

This is another of my favourite puddings, which I have been cooking since the early 1980s. If you don't have Crème de Cacao, then brandy or Cointreau will do. Just make sure that you eat this dish with plenty of ice cream.

140 g/5 oz caster sugar

55 g/2 oz unsalted butter

4 rings of fresh pineapple, skin removed and 2 cm/¾ in thick

125 ml/4 fl oz Crème de Cacao

freshly ground black pepper

1 Place the sugar in a pan with just enough water to dissolve the sugar. Bring to the boil and cook until you have a nice caramel colour.

2 Heat the butter in a large frying pan until it starts to brown slightly.

3 Season the pineapple with a little black pepper on both sides and lay in the foaming butter. Cook on both sides until they have taken a little colour.

4 Add the liqueur and flame or boil for a few seconds, then add the hot caramel. Warm through and reduce slightly.

5 Serve warm, topped with vanilla ice cream and a little more syrup.

SERVES 4 | PREP 20 MINS | COOK 15 MINS

American-style Pancakes with Cherries

This classic American pudding is perfect for everybody. Apricots or peaches, tinned or fresh, work well in this recipe. Again, just experiment and enjoy yourself.

85 g/3 oz caster sugar
350 g/12 oz fresh cherries, pitted
a little cornflour or arrowroot, mixed with a little cold water
vegetable oil for frying
good-quality vanilla ice cream, to serve

Pancake Batter
200 g/7 oz self-raising flour
85 g/3 oz finely ground cornmeal or polenta
1 tbsp caster sugar
1/2 tsp salt
1 medium egg
about 320 ml/11 fl oz milk

1 Place the sugar, 200 ml (7 fl oz) cold water and cherries in a saucepan and bring to the boil. Simmer for 1 minute, then thicken lightly with the cornflour. Keep warm.

2 To make the pancakes, put the flour, cornmeal, sugar and salt in a bowl. Mix well. Add the egg and milk, and bring together with a wooden spoon.

3 Heat 1 tablespoon vegetable oil in a nonstick frying pan and add 2 or 3 spoonfuls of pancake batter to the pan. Let the mixture run in the pan.

4 After 2 minutes, flip over with a spatula and cook for a further 2 minutes. Remove the pancake from the pan and keep warm. Repeat the process until all the batter has been used.

5 Serve two warm pancakes with the cherry sauce poured over, topped with a large spoonful of vanilla ice cream.

Apricot Batter Pudding

Easy and tasty, that's all I can say. Just make sure that you butter the dish or use a nonstick pan, otherwise you are in trouble. Any tinned fruit will work in this pudding apart from strawberries or raspberries. A good tip is to leave the pudding to rest for a couple of minutes to cool slightly before eating. Not only is it very hot, but also the batter needs to rest slightly. I cooked this for Sir Cliff Richard and he loved it, even taking the recipe away with him.

50 g/2 oz unsalted butter	4 small eggs
100 g/3½ oz soft flour, sieved	275 ml/9 fl oz full-cream milk
2 pinches salt	2 x 410 g/14 oz tins apricots in syrup,
4 tbsp runny honey	well drained
100 ml/3½ fl oz apricot brandy	

1 Heat the butter in an ovenproof dish or nonstick frying pan until very hot.

2 Place the flour, salt, honey, brandy and eggs into a bowl and mix well. Gradually add the milk until you have a smooth batter.

3 Pour the batter into the heated dish or pan, dot with the apricots and place in a preheated oven at 180°C (350°F, Gas mark 4). Cook for 35–40 minutes until puffed and nicely coloured.

4 Serve hot with double cream or ice cream.

One-Pot Suppers

You don't have to forgo the taste factor when you produce these marvellous one-pot dishes. The only thing you are missing out on is a mountain of dirty pots and pans after you have eaten them. What could be simpler? Delicious and simple-to-make meals without having to face the dreaded washing up more complicated dishes can bring.

Squash Barley Hotpot

The traditional way of making hotpot is to casserole scrag end of lamb with a potato crust packed full of root vegetables. Here, I add black pudding and squash, the squash replacing swedes and turnips, and the black pudding to give the whole dish a peppery bite. Instead of scrag end I use neck chops – they have a little more meat on them and slightly less fat.

1 large carrot, chopped	115 g/4 oz good-quality black pudding
2 small onions, finely chopped	1 organic lamb or chicken stock cube
2 large cloves garlic, crushed	2 tablespoons flour
a little vegetable oil	4 large baking potatoes, peeled and sliced not too thinly
4 neck chops, about 450 g/14 oz in total	
280 g/9 oz raw squash, peeled and diced	butter, melted
55 g/2 oz pearl barley, soaked in water for at least 3 hours	salt and freshly ground black pepper

1 Brown the carrot, onion and garlic together in a touch of vegetable oil until they have a nice colour and have wilted. In a separate pan, brown the chops on both sides, also in a little hot oil, until nicely browned. Place in a baking dish, spread over the squash, carrot mixture and pearl barley, and season well with the salt and pepper. Top with the black pudding.

2 Dissolve the stock cube in 600 ml (1 pint) boiling water. Mix the stock and flour together, and pour over the chops so that you just cover them. Top carefully with the sliced potatoes and season well with salt and pepper. Brush the melted butter over the top.

3 Cover the baking dish with tightly fitting foil and place in a preheated oven at 180°C (350°F, Gas mark 4). Cook for about an hour, then remove the foil and return the pan to the oven for a further 45 minutes to an hour to brown the potatoes. You may need to increase the temperature slightly so that they become crisp on top.

4 This dish is best cooked and eaten when it has been left to cool for about 30 minutes. Pickled cabbage works perfectly with hotpot ... just tuck in.

Warm Pasta with Smoked Salmon, Broad Beans and Dill

This is a great supper dish which also makes a quick and easy lunch. Frozen broad beans are a steal and can be used straight from the freezer.

175 g/6 oz frozen blanched baby broad beans

3 tbsp olive oil

3 spring onions, sliced on an angle

2 tbsp freshly chopped dill

500g /1 lb dried fusilli pasta, cooked and drained

225 g/8 oz smoked salmon, cut into thin strips

1 tbsp lemon juice

salt and freshly ground black pepper

To Serve

sour cream

freshly chopped chives

1 Add the beans to a pan of boiling water and simmer for about 4 minutes, or until tender. Strain.

2 Heat the olive oil in a wok (don't let it get too hot), then add the spring onion and cook for a few seconds to soften. Add the dill and pasta, then season well with salt and pepper. Cook for about 3 minutes to heat through.

3 Add the hot broad beans to the pasta with the smoked salmon and toss to combine. Cook for another 1–2 minutes to warm through – be careful you don't overcook the salmon. Season well and add the lemon juice.

4 Serve the pasta in a deep bowl, topped with a spoonful of sour cream and chopped chives.

SERVES 6-8

PREP 10 MINS

COOK 15 MINS

Swedish Meatballs

Meatballs, or *sma kottbullar*, are a real staple for the Swedes. They can be served with the creamy sauce as either a starter or a main, or without the sauce as part of a traditional *smörgasbord*.

450 g/1 lb lean minced beef	salt and freshly ground
1 small onion, very finely chopped	black pepper
1 large potato, peeled and grated	
4 tbsp dry breadcrumbs	**For the Sauce**
1 medium egg, beaten	1 tbsp flour
4 tbsp freshly chopped parsley	250 ml/8 fl oz single cream
2 tbsp vegetable oil	salt and freshly ground black pepper

1 Place the beef, onion, potato, breadcrumbs, egg, parsley and salt and pepper to taste into a bowl and mix well – probably best done on a machine.

2 Mould the meat mixture into balls the size of a walnut, place onto a plate and chill well.

3 Heat the vegetable oil in a frying pan until sizzling and add 6–8 meatballs. Cook on all sides until golden. Repeat the process until all the meatballs are cooked, then remove and keep warm.

4 To make the sauce, tip off most of the oil and add the flour. Stir well, to soak up the oil, before adding the single cream. Bring to the boil and stir well until thickened. Season well, then add the meatballs to the sauce, making sure to coat them well.

5 Serve with potato rosti.

Light Salmon Curry with Lemon Grass

A light, fragrant curry for everyday eating, the secret to which is not to overcook the salmon. Salmon is a big flavoured fish and will take to the curry well. Other seafood that works well includes monkfish, all prawns and cheaper fish such as coley, pollack, huss and skate.

150 ml/5 fl oz strong fish stock, boiling	pinch of sugar
1 tsp Thai green curry paste	4 x 175 g/6 oz salmon fillets, no skin
1 tsp tamarind paste	50 ml/2 fl oz creamed coconut
10 cm (4 in) stick lemon grass, bruised	4 tbsp freshly chopped coriander
4 shallots, very finely chopped	4 tbsp freshly chopped parsley
pinch of ground cumin	salt

1 Place a large pan on the stove and add the boiling stock, curry paste, tamarind paste, lemon grass, shallots, cumin and sugar. Bring to the boil and cook for 1 minute.

2 Add the salmon, cover and very gently simmer for 5–10 minutes, or until the fish is just cooked – do not overcook.

3 Remove the lid, check the seasoning and adjust if needed. Add the coconut, coriander and parsley, and serve in deep bowls.

Spicy Sausage Pilaf with Basil and Saffron

So simple to prepare and so delicious. It is unusual and comforting at the same time, with its use of spices, saffron and sausages. The fresh basil adds the final touch.

25 g/1 oz unsalted butter	1 medium red onion, chopped
4 or 5 large assorted sausages, cut into 1 cm/¹/₂ in pieces	1 garlic clove, crushed
	225 g/8 oz Basmati rice
2 tsp cumin seed	glass of white wine
2 tsp fennel seed	600 ml/1 pint strong chicken stock
1 tsp ground turmeric	4 tbsp freshly chopped basil
pinch of saffron threads	salt and freshly ground
1 tsp finely chopped fresh red chilli	black pepper

1 Heat the butter in a large ovenproof pan, add the sausages and cook for a couple of minutes so that they take a little colour.

2 Remove the sausages from the pan and add the cumin seed, fennel seed, turmeric, saffron and chilli. Cook for 2 minutes to release the flavour. Next, add the onion and garlic, and cook gently for about 5 minutes until soft.

3 Add the rice and coat well in the oils and butter, then add the wine, stock and sausages. Season well with salt and pepper, then bring to the boil, stirring.

4 Cover the pan with a tight-fitting lid and cook in a preheated oven at 180°C (350°F, Gas mark 4) for 14–16 minutes, or until the rice is tender.

5 Stir in the basil and serve.

SERVES **2** | PREP **10** MINS | COOK **35** MINS

Real Corned Beef Hash

Something like £5 million is spent by the NHS treating people for cuts sustained from opening corned beef tins, so be careful. Also, always chill the tin well before attempting to open – it makes a huge difference. My Auntie Joey, who lives near Preston, Lancashire, makes the best corned beef hash, and this is based on her recipe of years ago.

3 tbsp vegetable oil	3 tbsp Worcestershire sauce
1 large onion, finely chopped	250 g/8 oz chilled corned beef,
300 g/10 oz potato, cut roughly	cut into 3-cm/1¹/₄-in pieces
into 3-cm/1¹/₄-in pieces	salt and freshly ground
about 400 ml/14 fl oz beef stock, boiling	black pepper

1 Heat the vegetable oil in an ovenproof saucepan over medium heat. Add the onion and cook until it takes a little colour, then add the potato and stir together.

2 Add the beef stock, Worcestershire sauce and salt and pepper to taste. Bring back to the boil.

3 Cover, turn the heat down and simmer gently or pop into a preheated oven at 180°C (350°F, Gas mark 4) for 20 minutes until the potato is cooked and starting to break up. This is essential as it ensures that the stock is thickened by the potato breaking down, but still leaves some solids. You may need to add a touch more stock, if the potatoes dry out too much.

4 Add the chunks of corned beef, stir well and heat through for a further 15 minutes.

5 Finally, add the parsley and adjust the seasoning.

6 Serve with pickled red cabbage and pickled walnuts.

SERVES 4

PREP 20 MINS

COOK 55 MINS

Leek and Blue Cheese Lasagne

This dish is really nice not only as a hot main course, but also cut into squares and eaten as a great picnic snack. Lasagne usually has a lot of sauce or cream to keep it moist, but here I just use the leek and its buttery juices, which seems to work really well.

900 g/2 lb leeks, trimmed, rinsed well and finely chopped

115 g/4 oz unsalted butter, plus a little extra for greasing

9 fresh lasagne sheets, about 15 cm x 10 cm/6 in x 4 in

125 g /4 oz Danish blue cheese, crumbled

salt and freshly ground black pepper

1 Drain the leek in a colander and rinse again. Drain thoroughly once more – this is important so that when you cook the leek it does not 'boil' in any remaining water.

2 Heat the 115 g (4 oz) butter in a wok and, just as it is starting to turn brown, add the leek and season well. Cook for 5–6 minutes so the leek softens, but does not lose its colour. Sit a colander over a large bowl and tip in the leeks to drain while catching the juices.

3 Grease a 30 cm x 23 cm (12 in x 9 in) baking dish with the extra butter and lay 3 lasagne sheets in the bottom. Spread a third of the leek mixture over the lasagne, then sprinkle on a third of the blue cheese. Season with the salt and pepper. Cover with another 3 lasagne sheets and repeat the layers until you have used all the mixture and lasagne. Make sure that you season each layer well.

4 Add enough hot water to the reserved buttery leek juices to make it up to 350 ml (12 fl oz), then pour this around the edge of the dish. Cover the dish well with foil and bake in a preheated oven at 200°C (400°F, Gas mark 6) for about 45–50 minutes, or until tender and the juices have been absorbed.

5 Carefully remove the foil and pop back in the oven to brown the surface, then serve.

Pepperpot Beef with Kidney Beans

One of the best things about autumn is that it's a great time to enjoy a hearty stew. Here's one with a twist – the oranges and ginger give it a really different slant.

500 g/1 lb diced braising steak	1 x 410 g/13 oz tin kidney beans, drained and well rinsed
2 tbsp vegetable oil	
2 tbsp plain flour	1 small orange, cut into 6 wedges
1 tbsp tomato purée	1 beef stock cube, crumbled
1 small red onion, chopped	2 tbsp roughly chopped fresh coriander
1 red pepper, chopped	salt and freshly ground black pepper
1 yellow pepper, chopped	
1 heaped tbsp grated fresh ginger	**To Serve**
1 small fresh red chilli, seeds removed and chopped	sour cream (optional)
	freshly chopped parsley (optional)

1 Pat the meat dry using absorbent kitchen paper. Heat 1 tablespoon of the oil in a deep casserole dish or ovenproof pan. Add the meat and cook until browned all over. Sprinkle on the flour and stir in well with the tomato purée.

2 Heat the remaining 1 tablespoon oil in a frying pan. Add the onion, peppers, ginger and chilli, and cook gently until softened and golden brown. Tip the mixture into the casserole dish with the beef and stir together.

3 Place half the kidney beans in a food processor with an equal amount of cold water and blitz until smooth, then stir into the beef mixture. Add the orange segments, remaining beans, stock cube and coriander, and season with the salt and pepper. Heat to bring to the boil.

4 Cover dish with a tight-fitting lid and cook in a preheated oven at 180°C (350°F, Gas mark 4) for about 2 hours, or until the beef is tender.

5 Serve straight from the pot with a spoonful of sour cream and chopped parsley on top, if liked.

Hot Mango Tart

Again, quick and very simple. All you need is a hot oven, small nonstick pan, ripe mango and 15 minutes. For this to work properly, the oven has to be very hot.

---

1 ripe (but not too ripe) medium mango
55 g/2 oz caster sugar
30 g/1 oz unsalted butter

a circle of ready-made puff pastry, 12–14 cm/5–6 in in diameter, rolled extra thinly and pricked well with a fork

---

1 Place the mango on its end and cut the skin away with a sharp knife. Next pare away both halves, then slice the halves into thin slices, making sure to keep attached at one end (fanlike).

2 Place a small nonstick frying pan on the stove. Add the sugar and melt over a medium heat, stirring occasionally. When the sugar has turned to caramel, add the butter and mix well.

3 Remove from the heat and carefully lay the sliced mango on top of the bubbling caramel.

4 Place the pan back on the stove. Top the mango with the pastry and leave to bubble for 1 minute, then transfer the pan to a preheated oven at 200°C (400°F, Gas mark 6) and cook for 12–15 minutes, depending on your oven. The pastry will be slightly risen and golden.

5 Remove from the oven and invert the tart onto a warm plate. The hot buttery juices will run out, so do take care.

6 Serve straight away with ice cream or clotted cream.

SERVES 6-8

PREP 10 MINS

COOK 20 MINS

Hot Caramel and Peach Muffin

Great for the kids to help with, as it is very simple and they can do all the mixing. Just keep them away from the caramel.

185 g/6 oz caster sugar, plus 125 g/4 oz extra	200 ml/7 fl oz buttermilk
185 g/6 oz self-raising flour	30 g/1 oz unsalted butter, melted
pinch of salt	2 x 410 g/14 oz tins peaches in syrup, well drained
2 large eggs	

1 Heat the 185 g (6 oz) sugar in a cast-iron or nonstick frying pan – about 25 cm x 5 cm (10 in x 2 in) – until you have a nice light caramel, but do not let the sugar turn too dark in colour.

2 Meanwhile, place the self-raising flour, salt and extra caster sugar in a glass or ceramic bowl and mix well together. Add the eggs, buttermilk and melted butter, and stir well until you end up with a light but not thick and stodgy batter – you may need to add a touch of milk if the batter is too thick.

3 Place the peaches into the gently bubbling caramel and arrange carefully, then pour the muffin batter all over the hot peach and caramel mixture. The caramel will start to bubble over the edges of the muffin mixture. Don't worry about that – it's all part of the dish.

4 Place the whole pan in a preheated oven at 200°C (400°F, Gas mark 6) and cook for 15–20 minutes until the top of the muffin is golden brown and firm to the touch.

5 Remove from the oven and leave to set for about a minute, then carefully turn the muffin upside down onto a large plate.

6 Serve straight away with vanilla ice cream.

SERVES 4

PREP 10 MINS

COOK 4 MINS

Dried Fruits Steeped in Rosemary Syrup

A simple fruity dessert that will keep in the refrigerator for up to a week. The best way to eat this pudding is with vanilla ice cream or double cream.

250 ml/8 fl oz cold water	4 sprigs fresh rosemary
125 g/4 fl oz granulated sugar	350 g/12 oz mixed dried fruits such as
30 g/1 oz light soft brown sugar	pears, apricots, peaches etc.
juice and zest of 2 lemons	

1 Place the granulated and brown sugars and 250 ml (8 fl oz) cold water in a saucepan and bring to the boil. Once dissolved, remove from the heat and add the rosemary.

2 Pour the warm rosemary syrup over the fruits, cover and leave overnight.

3 Serve with vanilla ice cream or double cream.

Weekend Family Food

Weekends are the time where you can turn a meal into an occasion. Good food and good company are an important part of family life. You could choose a traditional Sunday roast or perhaps something more unusual. Whatever it is, the act of eating together becomes an enjoyable ritual.

SERVES 6 | PREP 20 MINS | COOK 30 MINS

Asparagus and Chicken Lasagne

Everybody loves a lasagne in one way, shape or form. Here the combination of asparagus and chicken is perfect. The ready-to-cook lasagne sheets you can buy now are very good indeed. This dish can also be made up, cooked and frozen for a later date.

40 g/1½ oz butter	600 g/1 lb 5 oz young English asparagus, trimmed and cut into 4 cm/1¾ in pieces
40 g/1½ oz plain flour	
600 ml/1 pint full-cream milk, boiling	2 large cooked chicken breasts, sliced into small pieces
pinch of grated nutmeg	
2 heaped tsp grain mustard	100 g/3½ oz sliced button mushrooms
4 x 18 cm/13 in ready-to-cook dried lasagne sheets	55 g/2 oz Parmesan cheese, freshly grated
	salt and freshly ground black pepper

1 Melt the butter in a saucepan and stir in the flour. Cook over a low heat for 2–3 minutes. Gradually add the hot milk, stirring all the time over a low heat, taking care not to let the sauce catch.

2 Once all the milk is added and the sauce has just boiled, add the nutmeg, salt and pepper to taste and mustard. Mix well.

3 To assemble the lasange, place about a third of the sauce in the bottom of a 24 cm x 14 cm (10 in x 6 in) lightly greased baking dish. Sprinkle over a little asparagus, sliced chicken and mushrooms, and season well. Add a layer of pasta with 2 of the lasagne sheets, then a third more sauce, asparagus, chicken and mushrooms. Top with the last 2 pasta sheets and cover with the last of the sauce, asparagus, chicken and mushrooms.

4 Sprinkle over the Parmesan cheese and a little salt and pepper. Bake in a preheated oven at 220°C (425°F, Gas mark 7) for 30 minutes, or until bubbling and nicely glazed. Leave to cool for 15 minutes or the whole thing will be too hot to eat.

5 Serve with garlic bread and chilled Sauvignon Blanc.

Lean Chicken and Tomato Curry

This is one of Fern's ideas, so I can't take the credit. It's delicious.

I large onion, chopped	2 tbsp sunflower oil
2 cloves garlic	3 skinless chicken breasts, free of any skin or fat, cut into 2 cm/1 in cubes
4 cardamom pods	
2 cm/³/₄ in piece of fresh ginger, peeled	150 ml/5 fl oz strong chicken stock
1 tsp chopped fresh red chilli	2 tbsp mango chutney
8 cherry plum tomatoes	juice of ¹/₂ lemon
¹/₂ tsp ground turmeric	4 tbsp freshly chopped coriander
¹/₂ tsp ground cumin	salt and freshly ground black pepper

1 Place the onion, garlic, cardamom, ginger, chilli, tomatoes, turmeric and cumin in a food processor and blitz to a paste.

2 Heat the oil in an ovenproof pan and add the chicken. Season well with salt and pepper, and brown slightly.

3 Add the onion paste, chicken stock and more salt and pepper. Bring to the boil, then pop the whole pan into a preheated oven at 220°C (425°F, Gas mark 7), uncovered, and cook for 20 minutes.

4 Remove from the oven. The mixture will have thickened slightly – if not, cook over a low heat for a couple of minutes.

5 Finally, stir in the mango chutney, lemon juice and coriander.

6 Serve with boiled rice.

Baked Gammon with Brown Sugar and Stout

This is an unusual way of cooking ham. It does take a bit of time, but is well worth the effort.

1 gammon joint, about 1.5 kg/3 lb, soaked overnight in cold water	1 small onion, halved
2 carrots, peeled	2 tbsp black peppercorns
1 small leek, rinsed well and cut in half	100 ml/3½ fl oz stout
4 sticks celery	140 g/5 oz dark brown sugar
2 bay leaves	100 g/3½ oz runny honey
	20 cloves

1 Place the gammon joint in a large pan. Cover with water and bring to the boil. Once boiling, simmer for 5 minutes, then taste. If the water is salty, then discard and start again. If not, add a little salt to taste.

2 Add the carrot, leek, celery, onion, bay leaves and black peppercorns. Lower the heat and simmer, uncovered, for bang-on 2½ hours. You may need to top up with boiling water from time to time to keep the ham covered. Turn off the heat and leave to rest.

3 Drain the gammon well and remove the strings, then cut off the skin and score the fat.

4 Warm the stout, sugar and honey until thick and syrupy. Keep warm.

5 Place the ham into a clean nonstick tray, spike with the cloves and pour over a little stout mixture. Bake in a preheated oven at 220°C (425°F, Gas mark 7) for 15 minutes. Keep spooning the stout mixture over the gammon periodically until you end up with a beautifully glazed joint.

6 Remove from the oven and leave to cool slightly, lift off and place on a ham spike or large, clean plate.

7 Serve warm with relish and creamed potatoes.

Tasty Cottage Pie

Strictly speaking, you should use beef for cottage pie and lamb for shepherd's pie, but to be honest with you I really don't care what meat I put in a pie like this. The secret is to get a full-flavoured, beautifully crunchy-topped comfort food.

1 small onion, chopped	1 medium aubergine, about 350 g/11 oz, sliced into thin rings
1 tsp fresh thyme leaves	
500 g/1 lb lean lamb mince	about 1 kg/2 lb cooked potatoes, mashed and kept warm
4 heaped tbsp plain flour	
2 tbsp tomato ketchup	200 ml/7 fl oz warm milk
1 tbsp Worcestershire sauce	100 g/3½ oz melted butter
350 ml/12 fl oz lamb	1 tsp paprika
or chicken stock	pinch of curry powder
6 tbsp olive oil	salt and freshly ground black pepper

1 Heat the vegetable oil in a saucepan. Add the onion and thyme, and cook for 5 minutes to colour slightly, then add the mince and also colour slightly. Next, add the flour and let the bottom catch slightly, before adding the ketchup and Worcestershire sauce. Mix well. Pour in the stock and bring to a very low simmer. Cook for 10 minutes.

2 Heat the oil until sizzling and cook the aubergine on both sides for minute or two to colour and soften. Drain and set aside.

3 Place the warm potato mash into a bowl and add the milk, butter, paprika and curry powder. Season with salt and pepper.

4 Place half the mince into a baking dish – about 30 cm x 20 cm (12 in x 8 in). Lay the cooked aubergine over the top, then add the rest of the mince. Pipe or spread the mash over the top. Allow to cool and wrap well in cling film before freezing.

5 To cook, remove from the freezer and defrost well. This is best done overnight in the refrigerator. Place in a preheated oven at 220°C (425°F, Gas mark 7) for 35 minutes, or until very hot and glazed. Serve hot.

Cashew and Mushroom Bake

A few years ago, this type of food was frankly a bit of a joke. But with a little care and attention, you can produce a very nice, flavourful supper for vegetarians and meat eaters alike.

2 tbsp olive oil	1 tbsp freshly chopped oregano
1 small onion, chopped	5 thick slices bread made into
1 tsp very finely chopped fresh red chilli	breadcrumbs, with crusts
2 cloves garlic, crushed	juice of 1 large lemon
2 x 410 g/13 oz tins chickpeas, drained	200 ml/7 fl oz vegetable stock
200 g/7 oz unsalted cashew nuts, chopped	salt and freshly ground black pepper
2 medium eggs, lightly beaten	225 g/8 oz flat mushrooms, chopped
1 tbsp freshly chopped rosemary leaves	a little vegetable oil

1 Heat the olive oil and soften the onion, chilli and garlic for 10 minutes.

2 Place the chickpeas and cashew nuts into a food processor and blitz until fairly smooth. Transfer to a bowl and add the egg, rosemary, oregano, breadcrumbs and lemon juice. Mix in the vegetable stock. Season well.

3 Cook the mushrooms in a little vegetable oil until lightly coloured. Cool.

4 Oil a 1 kg (2 lb) nonstick loaf tin, then place one-third of the chickpea mixture in the bottom, followed by a layer of cooked mushrooms. Smooth over a second layer of chickpea mixture. Spoon over the last of the mushrooms, finally topping with last third of the chickpea mixture.

5 Cover with foil and bake in a preheated oven at 200°C (400°F, Gas mark 6) for 45–50 minutes. Cool completely and freeze.

6 To serve, remove from the freezer, take off the foil and place into a preheated oven at 200°C (400°F, Gas mark 6) for 35 minutes until warm and slightly browned. Serve spooned or sliced, with a little green salad, crusty bread and garlic mayonnaise.

Traditional Prawn Cocktail

Here it is, that classic starter, the prawn cocktail. This is the traditional version – and very tasty it is, too.

225 g/8 oz full-fat mayonnaise	1/2 iceberg lettuce, finely chopped
6 tbsp tomato ketchup	1 tomato, thinly sliced
a couple of dashes of Worcestershire sauce	4 slices cucumber
dash of Tabasco sauce	4 wedges of lemon
350 g/12 oz cooked prawns, peeled and deveined	pinch of cayenne
	salt and freshly ground black pepper
	buttered brown bread, to serve

1 Place the mayonnaise, ketchup, Worcestershire sauce and Tabasco in a bowl and combine thoroughly. Season well with salt and pepper.

2 Add the prawns and carefully mix together.

3 Half-fill 4 tall glasses with the lettuce. Top with the prawn and mayonnaise mixture, then place some slices of tomato and a slice of cucumber in each glass, on top of the prawns. Finish with a lemon wedge and the cayenne.

4 Serve with buttered triangles of brown bread. A 'shell-on' prawn to garnish each cocktail always looks good.

SERVES
4

PREP
20
MINS

COOK
2½
HOURS

Traditional Roast Beef

This has to be the all-time Sunday lunch favourite. Just try cooking a forerib – the taste and tenderness of the meat make this the best joint to roast by far.

Roast Beef	Yorkshire Puddings
roast forerib of British beef on the bone, about 1.5 kg/3 lb	4 large eggs
4 potatoes, peeled and halved	225 g/8 oz flour
beef dripping or lard	600 ml/1 pint full-fat milk
	salt and freshly ground black pepper

1 Follow the tips for making the perfect Sunday roast and the method given for Roast Topside with New Potatoes, Garlic and Shallots on pages 113–14 and you should not go wrong.

2 To make the Yorkshire puddings, place the Yorkshire pudding tin in the oven to preheat, with a little dripping or lard in each of the cups. Beat the eggs together, then add the flour and half the milk. Mix to a smooth batter, add the last of the milk and season well. Pour the batter into the cups and return the tin to the oven. Cook for 40 minutes, or until well risen.

3 Serve with crisp roast potatoes (see tips), boiled carrots sweetened with a little sugar, buttered leeks and cauliflower cheese – and, of course, the Yorkshire puddings.

TIPS FOR THE SUNDAY ROAST

► The best roasting joints are sirloin and forerib. Sirloin is rather expensive, but beautifully tender and full of flavour. Forerib, which I prefer, is about half the price and again tender, succulent and juicy, with a good marbling of fat. If you don't like too much fat, ask your butcher to trim off the outside, but to me it's the best bit.

► I prefer to cook all my roasts on the bone, but you can roll and tie both joints of meat. Off the bone takes a fraction less cooking time.

► A good tip is to buy your joint of beef and place it uncovered in a refrigerator for 2–3 days so that the meat can really dry out. The darker the flesh, the better. The meat will tenderize and deepen in flavour.

- When cooking a joint of any meat, one of the secrets is to cook it in a moderate oven (180°C, 350°F, Gas Mark 4) for slightly longer. The meat then cooks evenly, rather than having an overcooked outside and raw inside. Also, once the joint is in the oven, you can forget about it.
- If you are going to serve roast potatoes with your joint, then I have a few tips for you. Use a variety such as Maris Piper, King Edward or Desirée, and peel, wash and blanch in boiling water for 2–3 minutes, or until the outsides are about to fall away. Drain well in a colander and either place around the joint or cook in a separate tray of hot dripping with plenty of salt and pepper. The secret is to only turn the potatoes over once, and then only when the bottoms are golden and crunchy.
- To add more flavour to the beef, you can rub in some dried mustard powder or even uncreamed horseradish, but you must make sure that you season well with salt and pepper.
- Roasting meats is probably the easiest of all cooking methods. All you need is the correct roasting joint, time, seasoning and resting time, and that's it. Now, I think even a man could do that in between having breakfast and kick-off at 3 p.m.
- Cold roast beef makes great sandwiches and pasta dishes.
- The juices in the tray make the best gravy, with a little help from some flour, stock, red wine and onions. I quite like a touch of Bisto at home.
- Once the joint is cooked, carefully remove from the tray and wrap loosely in tin foil to rest so that the meat relaxes and softens. A 3 kg (6 lb) joint of beef will keep warm for up to 45 minutes (believe me) and don't forget to add any juices to the finished gravy.
- If roasting meat off the bone, pop the joint on a bed of crushed foil so that the meat does not sit directly in the fat and fry. This also allows the juices to run out of the joint.
- Horseradish sauce is the most amazing thing. It's gorgeous, but do take care in your choice. It has to be good quality and, for me, the hotter it is the better.

TIPS ON YORKSHIRE PUDDINGS

It's up to you what vegetables you serve with the joint, but the two things you can not do without are roast potatoes (we have already touched on them) and Yorkshire puddings. Here are a few tips on the best Yorkies:
- Always season with salt and pepper at the last moment.
- Make sure that the oiled tins are very hot before adding the batter.
- Place the tray into a hot oven (200°C, 400°F, Gas mark 6) for about 15 minutes so that the puddings will rise quickly, then reduce the temperature to cook them through.
- The golden rule: when you think they are cooked, give them a further 5 minutes in the oven to set, then they should not collapse.

Plum Crumble with Clotted Cream

This recipe is a nice way to entice the family to eat plums. Some kids will not touch them raw, but seem to positively adore this crumble. Just make sure that they get plenty of crumble and cover it all in custard – seems to work every time.

	Crumble Topping
1 kg/2 lb soft, ripe plums	125 g/4 oz plain flour
125 g/4 oz unrefined sugar	100 g/3¹/₂ oz caster sugar
55 g/2 oz unsalted butter	125 g/4 oz ground almonds
225 g/8 oz clotted or thick double cream, to serve	175 g/6 oz cold unsalted butter

1 Place the plums into a stainless steel saucepan. Add the sugar, butter and 6 tablespoons cold water. Cook until soft and pulpy – you may need to add a little more cold water. Keep warm.

2 Process the flour, sugar. almonds and cold butter to a rough mixture, or combine the flour, sugar and almonds, and rub in the butter with your fingertips until the mixture resembles rough breadcrumbs.

3 Put the cooked plums into a ceramic baking dish roughly 25 cm (10 in) square and 4–5 cm (2 in) deep. Top with the crumble mixture. Place in a preheated oven at 220° (425°F, Gas mark 7) and cook for 20 minutes, or until slightly crunchy.

4 Serve warm with lashings of cream and custard.

Lower Calorie Prawn Cocktail

A prawn cocktail with a twist, the twist being that it is not laden with as many calories as the usual recipe. The perfect complement to your Lower Calorie Roast Beef with Yorskshire Puddings (see the recipe overleaf).

Cocktail Sauce
200 g/7 oz reduced-fat mayonnaise or crème fraîche, or mixture of both
2 tbsp tomato ketchup
4 tbsp passata
1 tbsp Worcestershire sauce
dash of Tabasco sauce

200 g/7 oz cooked prawns, peeled and deveined

175 g/6 oz poached fish such as cod, haddock or even salmon, flaked
½ iceberg lettuce, finely chopped
4 slices tomato
4 slices cucumber
4 wedges lemon
cayenne pepper
salt and freshly ground black pepper
Melba toast, no butter

1 To make the cocktail sauce, place the mayonnaise, ketchup, passata, Worcestershire sauce and Tabasco in a bowl. Mix together thoroughly and season well with salt and pepper.

2 Add the prawns and poached fish, and carefully mix together, taking care not to break up the fish too much.

3 Divide the lettuce among 4 tall serving glasses and half-fill each one, then top with the prawn and fish mixture. Finish with slices of cucumber and tomato, a pinch of cayenne and a wedge of lemon.

HINT
► A 'shell-on' prawn to garnish the finished cocktail always looks good.

SERVES	PREP	COOK
4	**40** MINS	**75** MINS

Lower Calorie Roast Beef with Yorkshire Puddings

If you love roast beef and you are on a lower calorie diet, then this recipe is ideal. You can have all the flavour with far fewer calories. Just remember, it's not what you eat, but how much!

rolled sirloin of British beef, about
3.5 kg/7^1/$_2$ lb, with half the fat removed

4 tbsp grapeseed oil

2 tbsp English mustard powder

500 g/1 lb new potatoes, well scrubbed

6 sprigs fresh mint

8 carrots in a bunch, halved lengthways

2 tbsp olive oil

4 medium courgettes, cut on the angle
into slices 1 cm/^{1}/$_2$ in thick

2 cloves garlic, crushed

salt and freshly ground black pepper

Yorkshire Puddings

8 tbsp grapeseed oil

2 large eggs

115 g/4 oz plain flour

300 ml/^{1}/$_2$ pint skimmed milk

salt and freshly

ground black pepper

Green Salad with Dressing

1 tbsp Dijon mustard

2 tbsp sherry vinegar

pinch of sugar

2 tbsp olive oil

2 tbsp grapeseed oil

salt and freshly ground
black pepper

salad leaves, including
rocket, watercress and
endive (about 250 g/8 oz)

1 Roll up a large piece of foil into a large ball, then flatten. Smear the rolled sirloin with the grapeseed oil, then season well all over with the mustard and salt and pepper. Place on the foil. Pop in a preheated oven at 220°C (425°F, Gas mark 7).

2 Meanwhile, place the potatoes on to boil on the stove with a few pinches of salt and the sprigs of mint.

3 Heat the remaining 2 tablespoons grapeseed oil in a griddle pan, add the carrots and season well. Place the carrots in the hot oven and cook for 20 minutes until soft but not overcooked. Keep warm.

4 When the carrots are cooked, make the Yorkshire puddings. Place the Yorkshire pudding tin in the oven to preheat, with 1 tablespoon each of the rapeseed oil in 8 cups. Beat the eggs together, then add the flour and half the milk. Mix to a smooth batter, add the last of the milk and season well.

5 Pour the batter into the 8 cups and return the tin to the oven. Cook for 30–40 minutes, or until well risen (always allow an extra 5 minutes when you think they are cooked – this should ensure that they do not collapse). If necessary, turn the oven down to 200°C (400°F, Gas mark 6) after the first 20 minutes, so that the puddings do not catch. You need the big heat for the rise, as it were, then a cooler heat to set the batter.

6 Heat the olive oil in a wok and cook the courgette for 2–3 minutes. Add the garlic and warm through. Season well with salt and pepper.

7 Finally, to make the salad, place the Dijon mustard, vinegar, sugar, salt and pepper into a bowl and whisk well. Gradually add the oils, whisking as you do so until they emulsify. Let down with a touch of water if necessary, so that you end up with a nice coating consistency. Place the salad leaves in a large serving bowl, pour over the dressing and toss through.

8 Remove the beef from the oven and cover with foil and leave to rest for about 20 minutes.

9 To serve, slice the beef and serve accompanied by the Yorkshire puddings, new potatoes, roasted carrot, courgette and green salad.

HINT
► The only real problem I have encountered was with the Yorkshire puddings. I have tried to make them with only 1 egg yolk and 3 whites, but unsuccessfully. Even with 2 and 2 I had poor results, so I have come to the conclusion that, rather than eating 3 or 4 Yorkshires, you should just eat one!

Plum Crunch

An alternative to the traditional plum crumble with rich clotted cream, this dessert may taste just as sinful, but is far easier on the waistline and therefore on your conscience.

900 g/1³/₄ lb soft, ripe Victoria plums, halved and stones removed

175 g/6 oz unrefined sugar

2 tbsp cornflour, slaked in a little water

50 g/2 oz plain flour

80 g/2¹/₂ oz unsalted butter, cold

125 g/4 oz digestive biscuits (8 biscuits)

200 g/7 oz muesli (Jordan's Original is perfect for this)

Custard

600 ml/1 pint skimmed milk

4 tbsp custard powder

sugar to taste

1 Place the plums into a stainless steel saucepan. Add the sugar and 6 tablespoons cold water. Cook until soft and pulpy – you may need to add a little more cold water. Thicken slightly with the cornflour paste and keep warm.

2 Process the digestive biscuits, flour and cold butter. Add the muesli and just bring together.

3 Put the cooked plums into a ceramic baking dish roughly 25 cm (10 in) square and 4–5 cm (2 in) deep. Spread the crunch topping over the top. Place in a preheated oven at 220° (425°F, Gas mark 7) and cook for 20 minutes, or until slightly crunchy.

4 Make the custard in the normal way, sweeten to taste with a little sugar and serve with the pudding.

Roast Topside with New Potatoes, Garlic and Shallots

Most of the time we roast the most expensive cuts of meat, but there are a few that are very good indeed and don't cost quite so much. Here is a prime example. As long as the meat has been properly hung, topside is very good and cheaper than sirloin and forerib. Apparently 70 per cent of British households still eat a Sunday roast beef on a regular basis, winning out by far over chicken and pork.

piece of topside with no added fat, about 800 g/1½ lb, rolled and tied	6 cloves garlic, unpeeled with the root end sliced off
30 g/1 oz good beef dripping or vegetable oil	olive oil
500 g/1 lb baby new potatoes	4 heaped tbsp roughly chopped flat-leaf parsley
16 small shallots, peeled	salt and freshly ground black pepper

1 Place the topside on a piece of scrunched-up foil and season well with salt and pepper. Smear over the dripping, pop into a preheated oven at 185°C (360°F, Gas mark 6–7) and set the timer for 45 minutes.

2 Pour 90–125 ml (3–4 fl oz) olive oil into a separate pan and warm in the oven. When hot, carefully place the baby potatoes, shallots and garlic in the pan. Season well with salt and pepper, cover tightly with foil and pop into the oven along with the beef. These will steam in their own juices in the amount of time the beef takes to cook.

3 If you like your beef pink, remove from the oven after about 45–50 minutes and rest for 15–20 minutes. If you like your beef well done, allow a further 20 minutes of cooking time. The secret to any roast meat is to leave for a period of time to rest and relax. Not only will the meat be slightly easier to carve, but also it will also appear to be more tender due to the muscle fibres relaxing.

4 When the potatoes are cooked, remove from the oven, take off the foil and stir in the parsley. Slice the meat and pile the potatoes, garlic, and shallots around. Serve with gravy and good old Yorkies.

HINTS AND TIPS
▸ Any leftover meat is perfect in sandwiches with plenty of horseradish and crisp lettuce.
▸ Strips of cold beef mixed with a little mayonnaise, soy and Worcestershire sauce and a little chopped onion make a great starter or snack.
▸ Make sure that you keep all the pan juices for the gravy. Add a little red wine and stock, and reduce slightly. Thicken with a little cornflour or arrowroot, but not too much.
▸ It's always best to leave a joint this size to rest for 20 minutes, covered, before you slice and serve. Not only will the meat be juicier, but it will also be slightly more tender.
▸ Always use beef dripping for roasting vegetables with beef. It's the only way to get full flavour and decent crisp roast potatoes.

Spicy Grilled Lamb Chops with Soft Onions

Lamb chops are ideal for coating with bastes and marinades, easy to cook and easy to eat. Our kids seem to love chops and can't wait to pick up the bones and gnaw them.

12 British lamb chops, well trimmed	2 pinches ground cloves
4 large red onions, peeled and sliced crossways, but with rings intact	1 tsp English mustard powder
	1 tsp ground allspice
150 ml/5 fl oz good-quality olive oil	1 Cox apple, peeled, cored and very finely chopped
4 sprigs fresh rosemary	
4 sprigs fresh thyme	juice of 1 large orange
70 g/2½ oz soft dark brown sugar	a little arrowroot or cornflour (optional)
2 tbsp cider vinegar	salt and freshly ground black pepper

1 Lay the onion slices on a baking sheet – you can stack them 2 or 3 high if you need to. Drizzle over the olive oil and a good seasoning of salt and pepper. Add the rosemary and thyme.

2 Cover tightly with foil and place on the top of the stove to heat through, then pop in a preheated oven at 180°C (350°F, Gas mark 4). Cook for about 45 minutes, or until very soft and sweet. This is very important – the softer the better. You are basically steaming them in olive oil. When cooked, lift the onions off the tray and keep the flavoured oil for a salad dressing.

3 Place the sugar, vinegar, cloves, mustard powder, allspice, apple, orange juice and a little salt and pepper in a saucepan. Bring to the boil and simmer for a minute or two, or until the sauce is thick and syrupy. Thicken with a little arrowroot or cornflour, slaked in a little cold water, if liked.

4 Lay the chops on a grilling tray and season well. Baste with the thickened sauce – the sauce must be thick to coat the chops. Place under a very hot grill and cook for 4–5 minutes. The chops will glaze nicely.

5 Warm the onions over a medium heat, pile onto 4 plates and top with the chops, then pour over any cooking juices.

Chocolate and Banana Strudel with Ice Cream

Great for the kids to help with, as it is very simple and they can do all the mixing. Just keep them away from the caramel.

90 g/3 oz pecan nuts, roughly chopped	25 g/1 oz white chocolate, roughly chopped
3 ripe large bananas, roughly cubed	zest of 1 large lime
75 g/2$^1/_2$ oz bitter chocolate, roughly chopped	75 g/2$^1/_2$ oz unsalted butter, melted
	6 large sheets of filo pastry

1 Place the nuts, banana, chocolate and lime zest into a bowl and stir well.

2 Lay a tea towel onto a clean kitchen surface and lay 1 sheet of filo on top. Brush the melted butter over the filo, then lay another sheet of filo over the first one. Repeat until all 6 sheets have been buttered and layered on top of each other. Lay the banana filling in a strip near the top edge of the pastry.

3 Fold over the top end of the filo, then use the tea towel to roll up the strudel. Tuck each end under and place on a nonstick baking tray. Butter well and bake in a preheated oven at 220ºC (425ºF, Gas mark 7) until golden and crisp.

4 Remove from the oven and leave to cool for 10 minutes, then cut with a serrated knife on a slight angle.

5 Serve topped with good-quality chocolate ice cream.

Crêpes Suzettes

This real 1970s favourite is now again very trendy – and very hard to beat for the best-flavoured pancake dish around.

Batter	Sauce
100 g/3½ oz plain flour	275 g/9 oz caster sugar
2 eggs	50 ml/2 fl oz orange juice and finely
about 200 ml/7 fl oz milk	grated zest of 2 oranges
25 g/1 oz butter, melted	water
finely grated zest of 1 orange	25 ml/1 fl oz brandy
pinch of caster sugar	25 g/1 oz butter
pinch of salt	vanilla ice cream and double
oil for greasing	cream, to serve

1 To make the batter, place the flour in a large bowl. Crack in the eggs and beat together. Slowly add the milk to make a thin batter, then whisk in the melted butter, orange zest, sugar and salt. Cover and let stand for 1 hour.

2 Next, make the sauce. Stir the caster sugar in a pan over a low heat until the sugar turns to caramel. Carefully add the orange juice and 90 ml (3 fl oz) water – you may need to stand back as it is likely to spit. Stir in. Add the orange zest, brandy and butter, and keep warm.

3 Heat a little oil in a nonstick frying pan until the oil begins to smoke. Pour in just enough of the batter to cover the base of the pan and cook until set and just brown on the edges. Flip or turn over the crêpe and cook the other side until just set. Turn the crêpe out onto a plate and repeat until the remaining batter is used.

4 To finish, warm the sauce in a shallow sauté pan, fold the crêpes into quarters and place in the hot sauce to warm through. I like to serve these with vanilla ice cream and double cream.

SERVES 6 | **PREP 30 MINS** | **COOK 15 MINS**

Morello Cherry and Chocolate Pancake Cake

This is a delicious recipe and is not as sickly as it sounds. The crème fraîche cuts the richness perfectly. It also works well with pears, made in the same way, but substituting a very tangy lemon for the chocolate mousse. Make it in advance and chill well.

2 x recipe pancake mixture, made into 4 pancakes (see page 31)

2 large eggs

180 g/6 oz extra bitter chocolate, melted over a pan of hot water

200 ml/7 fl oz double cream, very lightly whipped

100 g/3$^1/_2$ oz crème fraîche

1 x 720 g/1$^1/_2$ lb jar pitted Morello cherries in syrup, drained well

cocoa powder

drinking chocolate

1 Line a 18 cm x 7 cm (7 in x 3 in) loose-bottomed deep cake tin with cling film, then pop in the bottom, so that the finished cake lifts out easily. Cut the 4 pancakes to fit the cake tin, then place one in the bottom.

2 Whisk the eggs and 3 tablespoons cold water over a pan of gently simmering water until thick and hot. Remove from the pan and cool slightly.

3 Add the hot chocolate to the egg mixture and whisk well, then add half the whipped cream and stir well. Now add the crème fraîche and remaining cream. Mix carefully.

4 Gently squeeze out the cherries to remove most of the juice – this will help the mousse to set firmly. Place a few cherries on the bottom pancake, cover with mousse, top with the second pancake and repeat the process with the other 2 pancakes, finishing with a pancake on top. Press down slightly, fold over the cling film and chill well, preferably overnight.

5 When chilled, lift out carefully and remove the cling film. Dust with drinking chocolate and cocoa powder mixed together. Cut out a nice wedge with a hot knife and serve with double cream.

Blistering Barbecues

The barbecue – eternal symbol of lazy
summer days and evenings. There is
something about cooking and eating al fresco
that makes everything taste that much better,
even the humble sausage. And you don't
need a huge back garden to take advantage
of a barbecue. A patio or balconies will
also work when you have the urge
to serve your food sizzling.

SERVES	PREP	COOK
4	15 MINS	50 MINS

Grilled Chicken with Spicy Peanut Sauce

The only way to prepare chicken drumsticks for the barbecue is to poach them gently first – this way you know that the chicken is cooked. All you need to do is to finish them on the grill. Easy.

	Spicy Peanut Sauce
8 chicken drumsticks, skin on	2 tbsp vegetable oil
1 carrot	1 small onion, chopped
1 onion, chopped	2 cloves garlic, finely chopped
I organic chicken stock cube	I x 340 g/12 oz jar crunchy peanut putter
1 tbsp sesame oil	1 tbsp maple syrup
1 tbsp Worcestershire sauce	a couple of dashes of Tabasco sauce
pinch of chilli powder	4 tbsp freshly chopped coriander
pinch of ground cumin	2 tbsp malt vinegar
salt and freshly ground black pepper	

1 First, place the drumsticks into a clean saucepan. Add the carrot, onion and stock cube, and cover with cold water. Bring to the boil, then turn down the heat so that the chicken is just simmering. Season well with salt and pepper, and cook gently for 45 minutes. The meat must be cooked, but not falling off the bone. Carefully strain and drain well. Allow to cool.

2 Place the chicken in a bowl and add the sesame oil, Worcestershire sauce, chilli powder and ground cumin. Mix well to coat the chicken. Chill well.

3 To make the peanut sauce, heat the vegetable oil in a saucepan and add the onion and garlic. Cook for 15 minutes to soften.

4 Now add the peanut butter, maple syrup, Tabasco, coriander, vinegar and enough cold water to make a sauce consistency. Warm the sauce through, but do not boil. Adjust the seasoning, cover and keep warm until needed.

5 Pat the drumsticks dry with absorbent kitchen paper. Place them on the hot bars of the barbecue and brown on all sides for about 10 minutes. Serve with the warm peanut sauce in a separate bowl.

Char-grilled Burgers with Bourbon Relish

Great barbie grub. The bourbon relish works well with most meats and some fish and seafood, such as salmon or prawns.

Bourbon Relish	1 red pepper, very finely diced
1/2 tsp Cajun spice	4 spring onions, very finely chopped
125 ml/4 fl oz bourbon	
100 ml/31/2 fl oz dark soy sauce	**For the Burgers**
2 heaped tsp Dijon mustard	700 g/1 lb 9 oz lean, good-quality British beef mince
150 g/5 oz tomato ketchup	
100 g/31/2 oz soft brown sugar	1 medium egg
1 tbsp freshly chopped rosemary leaves	1 tsp Cajun spice powder
	touch of Tabasco sauce
1 tbsp freshly chopped oregano	salt and freshly ground black pepper

1 Place all the ingredients for the bourbon relish except the peppers and onion in a bowl. Mix well before finally adding the pepper and onions. If possible, leave overnight so that the flavours develop.

2 To make the burgers, mix the mince, egg, Cajun spice powder and Tabasco together, then season well with salt and pepper. Mould into four large 2 cm (3/4 in) thick burgers and chill well until needed.

3 Cook the burgers on both sides under a preheated grill, or on a griddle or barbecue, until the juices run clear. Remove from the grill and spoon over a little sauce.

Grilled Burgers with Fruity Coriander Ketchup

Ketchups, or catsups, as they were known, date back to medieval times. These days they are commonly associated with America, but we were making mushroom catsup before the nation of the United States was heard of. This is a great recipe perfect for barbecued sausages, burgers and other meats. The secret is to make sure that the chicken stock is really strong. You could use any spiced fruit jelly, but avoid mint jelly as the flavour is too overpowering.

3 tbsp vegetable oil

2 tbsp black mustard seeds

1/2 tsp sweet paprika

1 glass dry white wine

1 clove garlic, crushed

1 x 230 g/8 oz jar spiced apple jelly with pimentos

300 ml/1/2 pint boiling water

1 1/2 preservative-free organic stock cubes

1 tbsp malt vinegar

a little cornflour, slaked in cold water

4 heaped tbsp roughly chopped fresh coriander

salt and freshly ground black pepper

6–8 beef burgers

1 Heat the vegetable oil, add the mustard seeds and paprika, and cook over a low heat for 2 minutes. Add the white wine, garlic and apple jelly, breaking up the jelly with a whisk. Heat until dissolved.

2 Next add 300 ml (1/2 pint) boiling water, the stock cube, a touch of salt and pepper, and the vinegar. Turn up the heat and simmer for 10–15 minutes.

3 The mixture will thicken quite considerably. Keep tasting and, when you are happy with the strength, slightly thicken with the cornflour. Don't go overboard – all you want to do is just hold the sauce. I normally find that you will end up with about 500 ml (16 fl oz) of finished, thickened sauce. Pour into a bowl or jug, add the coriander and adjust the seasoning.

4 Grill the burgers until well done – probably 6–10 minutes – and serve with the ketchup spooned over liberally.

SERVES	PREP	COOK
4	10 MINS	10 MINS

Grilled Courgettes with Mango Relish

There are two types of courgettes: yellow and green. Yellow courgettes, for some strange reason, are double the price of the green ones. The secret is to make sure that you wash them well as they can be very gritty. Do not overcook them. It's best to leave them slightly undercooked so that they retain their crunchy texture. Season well with salt and pepper and just enough oil to make the salt and pepper stick to the vegetable. This stops the coals flaring and causing too much smoke. The dressing is ideal not only for grilled vegetables, but also fish and white meats. Tinned mango works very well and is good if you cannot get hold of a fresh ripe one.

4 medium courgettes, lightly oiled and seasoned well with salt and pepper

Mango Relish
1 small mango or 1 x 410g (13 oz) tin mango slices in syrup
6 mint leaves

$1/2$ tsp ground cumin
3 tsp lemon juice
2 tbsp white wine vinegar
sea salt and freshly ground black pepper
4 tbsp freshly chopped parsley
4 tbsp freshly chopped coriander
250 g/8 oz natural yoghurt

1 To make the relish, place all the ingredients into a blender and blitz for 1–2 minutes.

2 Place the courgettes on the hot bars of the grill or barbecue, and turn occasionally until lightly browned. Cook for 2–3 minutes before turning to ensure an even colour.

3 Remove from the barbecue and cut into 2 or 3 long slices. Serve the mango relish separately.

SERVES 6-8	PREP 15 MINS	MARINATE 2 HOURS	COOK 2 HOURS

Butterfly Leg of Lamb, the Cheat's Way

Lamb is, I think, one of the best meats to cook on a barbecue. It's quick and easy, and marries very well with all the marinades, spices and flavourings you can throw at it. I prefer my lamb nice and pink, but that's really up to you. The best way to cook this large piece of meat is to 'butterfly' – that's basically completely boned, then cut open and laid flat, simple! If you have a large kettle or gas barbecue, you can cook this joint a lot quicker, as you can place a lid over the meat, then turn the heat right down and cook evenly. If not, you can cheat. Start the lamb in a moderate oven, say, 180°C (350°F, Gas mark 4), for about 45 minutes, then transfer to the barbecue and finish off. This way you can completely control the cooking process, add the tasty barbecue flavour and get a beautiful, nicely browned and glazed result. Nobody will ever know, I promise. Just remember to pat the meat dry before placing on the bars to stop 'flare up' and the all too familiar burnt offerings.

5 tbsp creamed horseradish

3 tbsp redcurrant jelly

2 tbsp wholegrain mustard

1 x 2.5 kg (5 lb) leg of British lamb, boned, opened and laid flat

4 cloves garlic, cut into thin slivers

4 tbsp olive or vegetable oil

salt and freshly ground black pepper

1 Mix together the horseradish, redcurrant jelly and mustard. Season well with a little salt and pepper, and set aside.

2 Make 15–20 small incisions in the lamb with a sharp knife. Insert the garlic slivers into the incisions, pushing well in.

3 Spread the olive oil over the lamb, season well with black pepper and leave to marinate for 2 hours.

4 If you are starting in the oven, place the lamb in a baking dish and cook in a preheated oven at 180°C (350°F, Gas mark 4) for 40 minutes. Remove from the oven and spread the horseradish mixture over the meat. Carefully place on the hot bars of the barbecue and cook over a medium heat for 20 minutes until nicely glazed. Turn over and continue to cook for a further 20 minutes. Take care not to burn the joint.

5 If you are using the barbecue method, place the marinated leg of lamb on the hot bars and gently brown on both sides. Cover with the lid and slowly cook for 1 hour, turning occasionally. Once the hour is up, spread over the horseradish mixture and glaze over the hot coals.

6 In both cases, remove from the bars and leave to rest, covered in foil, for 20 minutes.

7 Slice and serve with more redcurrant or mint jelly and cooked new potatoes at room temperature.

SERVES	PREP	MARINATE	COOK
4	**10** MINS	**2** HOURS	**9** MINS

Grilled Salmon with Fresh Ginger and Hoisin

Salmon is perfect for the barbecue. It's easy too cook, cheap and tastes great. The best cut to use is the tail fillets, as they are even cheaper. Make sure that the fish is scaled, but with the skin still on. This helps to protect the flesh from the heat. You can then eat the fish from the crisp skin easily. These subtle Chinese flavourings are perfect with fish. All you need with the salmon is a few new potatoes or some grilled summer vegetables.

4 salmon tail fillets, about 175 g/6 oz each	2 tbsp vegetable oil
6 tbsp good-quality hoisin sauce	1 tsp caster sugar
55 g/2 oz fresh ginger, finely chopped or grated*	salt and freshly ground black pepper

1 The day before, place the salmon fillets into a ceramic or glass dish.

2 Put the hoisin sauce, ginger, vegetable oil and sugar into a separate bowl. Season with salt and pepper, and mix well. Spoon over the salmon, cover and place in the refrigerator to marinate for 2 hours or overnight if you wish.

3 When the barbecue is hot, place the salmon on the hot bars skin-side down. Slowly cook until the flesh starts to turn a milky white on the edge. At this point, you can whip them over – I normally just leave them for a few more minutes. If you have a kettle barbecue, then just put the lid down. Salmon is always best eaten slightly undercooked.

4 Serve with spring onions and watercress.

* If grating, make sure that you keep all the juice.

Key Lime Pie

Calories or what, but who cares? This is very rich ... and very, very good. You've been warned!

1 x 24 cm x 3 cm/10 in x 1¼ in sweet pastry case, baked blind	225 g/8 oz crème fraîche
	60 g/2 oz caster sugar
1 x 397 g/13 oz tin condensed milk	
450 g/1 lb cream cheese	**To decorate**
juice of 4 large limes	8 lime slices, peeled not pared
finely grated zest of 2 limes	icing sugar

1 Whip the cream cheese, condensed milk and lime juice until thick and glossy. Add the zest and stir well. Spoon into the cooked pastry shell and smooth out.

2 Whisk the crème fraîche and caster sugar together until light. Spread over the top of the pie, then chill well for at least 1 hour.

3 To decorate, place the lime slices around the edge of the tart and dust with a little icing sugar. Cut and serve.

Fresh Blackcurrants with Vanilla Ice Cream

The wonderful thing about currants, whether they are black, white or red, is that they are delicious either fresh or frozen and defrosted. So, if you get a real glut, just freeze them flat on trays and bag up when they are frozen. This makes it much easier to remove from the freezer when you require them. In fact, I think that fresh frozen, defrosted and used makes a better sauce or coulis. Here is a nice idea using fresh blackcurrants. Quick and simple, and, although not a barbecue idea, great for when all the cooking is over.

350 g/12 oz fresh blackcurrants, topped and tailed	zest and juice of 1 lemon
75 g/2¹/₂ oz caster sugar	3 tbsp fruit juice such as grape
	good-quality vanilla ice cream

1 Place the blackcurrants in a stainless steel, ceramic or glass bowl. Lightly crush with a potato masher or fork.

2 Sprinkle over the sugar, lemon juice and zest, and fruit juice. Leave to stand for 1 hour covered with cling film, then chill well, preferably overnight.

3 All the juice is drawn out of the blackcurrants and turns into a delicious, fresh compote – just spoon it over ice cream. Even better, if you are using the frozen variety, simply defrost and follow the recipe, the sauce will be much darker.

Mrs King's Haymakers Lemonade

As a teenager, I worked on George King's farm, and every year we would get the hay in the hard way with his son Andrew. By that I mean by hand and pitchfork. As you can imagine we did work up a real thirst. Mrs King, the farmer's wife, made this wonderful lemonade – very thirst quenching. All the credit has to be hers. Thanks for great memories.

2 large lemons, peeled with a vegetable peeler	25 g/1 oz citric acid
900 g/2 lb granulated sugar	1.75 litres/3 pints boiling water

1 Squeeze the lemons and put the juice into a large bowl, along with the lemon peel, sugar and citric acid.

2 Pour on the boiling water and stir well until dissolved.

3 Cover and leave to cool completely, then strain through a fine sieve.

4 This recipe makes about 2.5 litres (4 pints). Bottle and dilute as necessary, adding plenty of ice cubes and sliced lemon.

SERVES	PREP	COOK
4-6	**5** MINS	**3** MINS

Iced Sweet Tea

This is an American speciality. I think they make it a little too sweet, so here is my version. The secret is to infuse the tea for only 1–2 minutes. After that, the leaves release too much tannin. I also add fresh lemon, orange and mint to give a nice kick. This is a great non-alcoholic drink and even the kids may like it.

3 breakfast tea bags

3 Earl Grey tea bags

1.5 litres/2^1/$_2$ pints boiling water

zest of 1 orange and 1 lemon, removed with a vegetable peeler

4–6 tbsp caster sugar

fresh mint

ice cubes

1 Place the tea bags into a jug and pour over the boiling water. Leave to infuse for 2 minutes, then remove the tea bags.

2 Add enough sugar to sweeten. It's really up to you how much you put in – I generally find 4–6 tablespoons is plenty. Cool completely.

3 Add the orange and lemon zest, cover and chill well overnight.

4 Serve in tall glasses with a few extra slices of lemon and orange, a few leaves of fresh mint and plenty of ice cubes.

Feasts and Celebrations

Children's birthdays, bonfire night,
Halloween – special occasions demand
special occasion food. A mix of irresistible
finger food and appealing hearty dishes, and
of course those all-important sweet treats
and spectacular desserts, will go down very
well with children and adults alike.

Worm Pasta with Blood Sauce

Sometimes when it comes to kids, the more ghoulish, the better. And this dish certainly fits the bill. The black pasta doused in its blood-red sauce will appeal to the most macabre child.

2 tbsp olive oil	2 tsp vinegar
1 small onion, finely chopped	225 g/8 oz black tagliatelle, cooked and
1 x 400 g/13 oz tin chopped tomatoes	tossed in a little olive oil
1 tbsp tomato purée	cheese, grated, for serving
2 tsp caster sugar	salt and freshly ground black pepper

1 1 Heat the olive oil in a small saucepan until sizzling. Add the onion and cook for 3 minutes.

2 Next add the tomato, tomato purée, sugar and vinegar, and season to taste with salt and pepper. Cook for about 15 minutes until the sauce is thick and tasty.

3 Adjust the seasoning, then blend or process. Keep warm.

4 Reheat the pasta 'worms' and pour over the 'blood' sauce.

Mashed Potato Ghosts and Dead Man's Fingers

This is a fun idea. The mashed potato ghosts are great fun to make and do look quite spooky, sitting alongside the 'dead man's fingers' perfectly.

Mashed Potato Ghosts	Dead Man's Fingers
potatoes, peeled and halved	chipolata sausages
a little milk	flaked almonds
sunflower seeds	tomato ketchup
beaten egg	
salt and freshly ground black pepper	

1 To make the ghosts, make mashed potatoes in the normal way, but don't add any butter. Return the potatoes to the pan to remove any excess moisture. Do not beat or the mash will become gluey.

2 Sieve or process the dry potatoes, then place in a bowl. Add a little salt and pepper. Mix well. Finally, add a touch of milk to make it easier to pipe. Using a plain 1-cm (¹/₂-in) nozzle, pipe small towers of puréed potatoes, making them gradually thinner as you get to the top. Place 2 sunflower seeds as eyes in the top of the ghost and brush with beaten egg. Place in a preheated oven at 220°C (425°F, Gas mark 7) to crisp up slightly.

3 To make the dead man's fingers, skewer 4 chipolatas onto a kebab stick. Cut off one of the fingers, say, the index, then grill. Place 3 flaked almonds in the ends of the 3 full chipolatas, to look like fingernails, then drizzle a little ketchup over the severed index finger.

4 Serve on a large plate with extra blood (ketchup) alongside the mashed potato ghosts.

HINT
You can use garnishing paste for the ghosts' eyes if you wish. This is a black paste used to decorate hams and salmon etc. Some delis and supermarkets now stock the paste.

Spider Cake

Very easy to prepare and with a quick icing top.

125 g/4 oz soft unsalted butter	125 g/4 oz bitter chocolate
125 g/4 oz caster sugar	125 ml/4 fl oz double cream
2 medium eggs, lightly beaten	white chocolate, melted
125 g/4 oz self-raising flour	1 marshmallow tea cake
chocolate chips	8 black pipe cleaners

1 Beat the butter and sugar together until very creamy and white.

2 Gradually beat in the egg, making sure that the mixture does not curdle.

3 Fold in the flour and chocolate chips.

4 Spoon the mixture into a buttered 24 cm (10 in) cake tin and bake in a preheated oven at 190°C (375°F, Gas mark 5) for 25–30 minutes until golden and well risen. Cool.

5 Next make the glaze. Melt the bitter chocolate over a pan of gently simmering water. Boil the cream separately and whisk into the melted chocolate off the heat. Leave to cool to room temperature.

6 To finish, place the cake on a wire rack, pour over the setting glaze and leave to cool completely.

7 Pipe a web of melted white chocolate on the top of the cake and feather lightly. To do this, make rings of the melted chocolate using a small piping bag fitted with a small, plain nozzle. Then, using a knife, run through the melted chocolate from the centre out to create a web effect.

8 Next make the spider by inserting the bent pipe cleaners into both sides of the tea cake, to look like legs. Pipe 2 eyes and large fangs on the front of the tea cake and place in the middle of the web.

9 That's it – just serve.

Web Jelly

Plastic spiders and flies can be added to this jelly to make it spookier, but only for slightly older children.

green jelly crystals, the greener the better

dark chocolate

vegetable oil

black 'ready roll' icing

1 Make the jelly in the normal way and set in a clear, shallow glass dish.

2 Melt the chocolate over a pan of simmering water. Remove from the heat and stir in a little vegetable oil. Do not add water or the chocolate will thicken and spoil straight away.

3 Pipe a web on the jelly using the melted chocolate, starting from the middle then working outwards until the whole jelly is covered. Then pipe lines out from the centre to form the stays of the web.

4 Finally, make a black witch's hat from the sugar paste and place in the centre of the web.

Creamy Fudge Fondue with Marshmallows

This is a great hit with the kids – quick, easy and very more-ish. I really enjoy this once in a while myself. It's just good fun and the kids will love it. Pieces of fresh and dried fruit are also very good with this sauce.

125 g/4 oz unsalted butter	juice and zest of I large lemon
190 g/6 oz soft brown sugar	200 g/7 oz marshmallows
600 ml/1 pint double cream	angel cake or Madeira cake, cubed

1 Place the butter, sugar and cream in a heavy pan and gently heat until the sugar dissolves.

2 Remove from the heat and stir in the lemon juice and zest, and mix well.

3 Stick long forks into the marshmallows and use to dip in the fondue. You can do the same with the cubes of angel cake.

SERVES 6-8   PREP 20 MINS   COOK 35 MINS

Pumpkin Cake

A good all-round afternoon tea cake which is simple, quick and great for Halloween celebrations.

175 g/6oz self-raising flour	140 g/5 oz caster sugar
1/4 tsp baking powder	200 g/7 oz tinned pumpkin purée
1/4 tsp bicarbonate of soda	3 tbsp milk
1 1/2 tsp mixed spice	1 large egg, beaten
1/2 tsp freshly grated nutmeg	icing sugar for dusting
50 g/2 oz unsalted butter	thick double or clotted cream

1 Line a 900 g/1³/₄ lb loaf tin (about 22 cm x 11 cm x 6 cm (11 in x 4¹/₂ in x 2¹/₄ in) deep) with greaseproof paper and grease well.

2 Mix together the flour, baking powder, bicarbonate of soda, mixed spice and nutmeg. Add the butter and rub in until mixture resembles fine breadcrumbs. Next, add the caster sugar and mix well.

3 Mix together the pumpkin, milk and beaten egg. Fold into the flour mixture, but do not overwork. Spoon into the prepared tin and bake in a preheated oven at 180°C (350°F, Gas mark 4) for 35–40 minutes until well risen.

4 Once the cake is cooked, remove from the oven and cool in the tin, then turn out onto a plate or board for cutting.

5 Dust with icing sugar and serve with thick cream.

Witches' Brew

Great way to involve kids in making their own food. The proportions are up to you, of course, but the weirder, the better in my view.

blackcurrant sorbet	cranberry juice
mango purée	red and black liquorice, to decorate

1 Place a ball of blackcurrant sorbet into a tall, thin glass.

2 Cover with the thick mango purée.

3 Top with cranberry juice and decorate the glass with red and black liquorice. You should see the colours beautifully.

4 Serve straight away.

Roasted Pumpkin and Cheddar Dip

Very simple, quick and seasonal.

350 g/12 oz roasted pumpkin (about 600 g/1¼ lb raw weight)	150 g/5 oz Cheddar, finely grated
100 g/3½ oz pumpkin seeds	4 tbsp mango chutney
1 large clove garlic, crushed	2 tbsp mayonnaise
2 tbsp extra virgin olive oil	4 tbsp good-quality olive oil
	salt and freshly ground black pepper

1 Roast the pumpkin on the skin for 35–40 minutes with a generous amount of olive oil and salt and pepper. Leave until completely cold.

2 Using a dessertspoon, carefully spoon out the flesh, paring it away from the skin, and place it in a large bowl. Gently mash with a potato masher until you have a chunky purée.

3 Simply add the rest of the ingredients and stir thoroughly. Season well with salt and pepper. It's best to leave for a couple of hours at ambient temperature so that the dip takes on a full flavour.

4 To serve, either spread onto warm baguettes or dip sausages in and eat.

SERVES	PREP	COOK
4-6	20 MINS	40 MINS

Autumn Vegetable Casserole

A great autumn warmer, its balance of all the flavours is terrific and it is a great partner with most roasts or simply on its own. The flavours brought out of autumn vegetables by casseroling are amazing. Most vegetables can be used in this dish – it's really up to you. The particular combination of sweet potato and pumpkin is a very good one. This is best made and left in the refrigerator overnight, then gently reheated to improve the flavour.

2 tbsp vegetable oil	100g creamed coconut, combined with
1 medium onion, finely chopped	275 ml/9 fl oz boiling water
1 heaped tbsp finely chopped ginger	1 vegetable stock cube
200 g/7 oz sweet potato, finely chopped	2 tsp Thai green curry paste
200 g/7 oz pumpkin, finely chopped	1 tbsp mango chutney
1 clove garlic, crushed	1 x 410 g/13 oz tin chickpeas
4 medium carrots in a bunch, unpeeled, washed well, stalks on and cut into 3 on the slant	200 g/7 oz fresh baby spinach
	4 heaped tbsp freshly chopped coriander
	salt and freshly ground black pepper

1 Heat the vegetable oil in a thick-bottomed casserole dish, then add the onion, ginger, sweet potato and pumpkin, and cook for 2–3 minutes until just coloured.

2 Add the garlic, carrot, creamed coconut, stock cube, curry paste, mango chutney and chickpeas, and stir to a gentle simmer.

3 Season well with salt and pepper, cover and place in a preheated oven at 160°C (325°F, Gas mark 3). Cook for 35 minutes.

4 Remove from the oven and stir in the spinach and coriander, and adjust the seasoning. Leave to rest for 10 minutes, to allow the spinach and coriander to wilt.

5 Serve accompanied by boiled red rice.

SERVES	PREP	COOK
4	**15** MINS	**1** HOUR

Refilled Baked Spuds with Bacon and Onion

As children, my brother and I loved these potatoes. This is real comfort food and served with baked beans they cannot be beaten. Nowadays baked spuds are all the rage and I still really enjoy them. Fern often cooks them for my supper ... if the football is on.

4 large baking potatoes, well washed
6 rashers British streaky dry-cured bacon, chopped into small pieces
1 onion, roughly chopped

2 tbsp vegetable oil
125 g/4 oz good-quality Cheddar, grated
salt and freshly ground black pepper

1 Place the potatoes in a preheated oven at 220°C (425°F, Gas mark 7) and bake for 1 hour, or until soft with crunchy skins.

2 Meanwhile, heat a saucepan and add the bacon. Cook over a low heat without any oil (there will enough fat in the bacon) until crispy.

3 Remove the bacon from the pan with a spoon and add the onion and vegetable oil, then cook for a further 10 minutes until soft and slightly browned. Return the bacon to the same pan and stir well.

4 Remove the potatoes from the oven and cut in half lengthways. Spoon the hot potato flesh into a bowl, making sure that you keep the skins intact.

5 Add the bacon and onion mixture to the potatoes, season with a little salt and pepper, and mix carefully. Do not purée.

6 Spoon the mixture back into the shells, piling nice and high. Sprinkle over a little grated cheese and more black pepper. Return to the oven or place under a hot grill until the cheese is lightly browned.

7 That's it. Simple, but really great to eat. And all you need really is a little brown sauce to transform it into a good TV dinner.

SERVES 4-6

PREP 10 MINS

COOK 50 MINS

Creamy Pumpkin and Mushroom Soup

Do take the time to roast the pumpkin first, as this will make all the difference to the end flavour of the soup. All you need is a good glug of extra virgin olive oil and plenty of black pepper to finish. The consistency varies quite a bit, so adjust if needed.

450 g/15 oz fresh pumpkin, skin left on and seeds removed, cut into large chunks
4 tbsp vegetable oil
125 g/4 oz unsalted butter
1 small onion, chopped
2 cloves garlic, chopped
1 level tsp mild curry powder

125 g/4 oz button mushrooms, roughly chopped
1.2 litres/2 pints well-flavoured chicken or vegetable stock
150 ml/5 fl oz double cream
100 g/3^1/$_2$ oz pumpkin seeds
extra virgin olive oil
salt and freshly ground black pepper

1 Drizzle the pumpkin with the vegetable oil and season well with salt and pepper. Place in a preheated oven at 200°C (400°F, Gas mark 6) and cook for 30 minutes to soften and colour a little. This helps to intensify the flavour.

2 Meanwhile, heat the butter in a large saucepan and add the onion, garlic and curry powder. Cook for 10 minutes to soften and colour slightly. Add the mushrooms and cook for a few minutes before adding the chicken stock. Bring to the boil, then simmer.

3 Take the pumpkin out of the oven and carefully remove the hot flesh from the skin with a spoon – I use rubber gloves for this. Place straight into the hot stock, season well and simmer for 15 minutes, or until the onion is soft.

4 Blend or process until liquid, then pass through a fine sieve before returning to the pan. You may need to add a little boiling stock to thin slightly, as the consistency of the soup will vary with each pumpkin.

5 Add the cream and pumpkin seeds, and adjust the seasoning. Serve hot with crusty French bread and a dash of extra virgin olive oil.

SERVES 4-6 **PREP 15 MINS** **COOK 10 MINS**

Devil Sauce

Ideal for grilled sausages. In fact, it is ideal for any grilled meat.

55 g/2 oz unsalted butter	1 heaped tbsp mango chutney
1 small onion, finely chopped	1 tbsp Worcestershire sauce
1 clove garlic, finely chopped	275 ml/9 fl oz strong beef stock
pinch of chilli powder	a little cornflour slaked in cold water
dash of Tabasco sauce	salt and freshly ground
2 tsp vinegar	black pepper

1 Heat the butter in a pan. Add the onion and garlic, and cook for 2–3 minutes.

2 Now add the remaining ingredients except for the cornflour and simmer for 3–4 minutes.

3 Thicken slightly with the cornflour and adjust the seasoning with salt and pepper. Keep warm.

4 Serve warm with grilled sausages. This sauce will keep in the refrigerator for up to 1 week.

BONFIRE SAUSAGE SAUCE
Another sauce ideal for a barbecue or indeed for bonfire night. Place 225 ml (8 fl oz) tomato ketchup, 2 tbsp Worcestershire sauce, 55 g (2 oz) soft brown sugar, 2 tsp dried mustard powder, 25 g (1 oz) runny honey, 3 tbsp malt vinegar, 1 tsp Cajun spice, 1 tsp ground cumin and 2 pinches chopped fresh red chilli in a saucepan, add 125 ml (4 fl oz) cold water and bring to the boil. Reduce the heat and simmer gently for 2 minutes, or until slightly thickened. Adjust the seasoning with salt and pepper, and serve hot or cold to accompany sausages or burgers.

Parkin

This is my mum's recipe and I'm assured its very good indeed by my dad. I can't stand ground ginger, so unfortunately it's out for me. Lancashire and Yorkshire both have recipes for parkin, but I'm not telling you which side of the Pennines this came from.

225 g/8 oz plain flour	280 g/9 oz black treacle
2 pinches salt	225 g/8 oz unrefined caster sugar
1 tsp ground ginger	180 g/6 oz unsalted butter
1 tsp mixed spice	1 tsp bicarbonate of soda
225 g/8 oz oatmeal	125ml/4 fl oz milk

1 Sift the flour, salt, ginger and mixed spice together. Add the oatmeal and stir well.

2 Melt the treacle, sugar and butter together until nice and runny.

3 Dissolve the bicarbonate of soda in the milk.

4 Pour the treacle mixture into the dry ingredients, then add the milk mixture. Carefully stir together and pour into a well-greased loaf tin about 20 cm x 25 cm (8 in x 10 in).

5 Cook in a preheated oven at 180°C (350°F, Gas mark 4) until well risen and firm, about 45 minutes. Cool and cut into large squares.

6 I like to serve this with either a cup of hot, strong tea or warm, with syrup custard.

MAKES 10 | **PREP 20 MINS** | **COOK 45 MINS**

Chocolate and Hazelnut Bonfire Brownies

Brownies are very easy to make. All they need is a long, slow cook to achieve the soft, moist inside. They also keep well for up to a week. I like to serve mine warm with hot fudge sauce and lots of ice cream. Here I use milk chocolate, but you can use bitter chocolate – just add a touch more sugar. The secret is not to overbeat the mixture once the flour is incorporated.

290 g/10 oz plain flour	3 medium eggs, lightly beaten
1 tsp baking powder	325 g/11 oz caster sugar
175 g/6 oz unsalted butter, cubed	a few drops of vanilla extract
250 g/8 oz milk chocolate	2 pinches salt
1 heaped tsp coffee granules dissolved in	175 g/6 oz toasted hazelnuts, crushed
1 tbsp hot water	icing sugar for dusting

1 Brush a 23-cm (11-in) square ceramic baking dish with melted butter and sprinkle with a little flour. Sift the flour and baking powder together.

2 Place the butter, chocolate and coffee into a bowl and melt over a pan of gently simmering water.

3 Meanwhile, beat the eggs, sugar and vanilla at high speed for about 2 minutes. Add the melted chocolate mixture slowly and mix well, then add the flour, salt and hazelnuts. Mix slowly until incorporated. Don't overwork.

4 Pour into the prepared baking dish and bake in a preheated oven at 180°C (350°F, Gas mark 4) for 45–50 minutes, or until risen and set. When a knife is inserted, the blade should come out with very slightly uncooked mixture. The brownies should be very moist and soft.

5 Cool in the dish, then turn out, cut into small squares and dust heavily with icing sugar. The brownies can then be reheated gently in a microwave or eaten cold. Serve with fudge sauce and ice cream or thick double cream, or eat them just on their own. Delicious.

Party Mix, the Alternative Nibble

It makes a change to have a different nibble to hand around at a party. There is a lot of one-upmanship in cooking – you will definitely get your friends asking about this little number.

sunflower oil

200 g/7 oz sweet potato, sliced very thinly on a mandolin

1 x 410 g/13 oz tin chickpeas, well drained and dried on absorbent kitchen paper

75 g/2¹/₂ oz semi-dried cherries

45 g/1¹/₂ oz crispy fried onion flakes (available from a deli or supermarket)

100 g/3¹/₂ oz sunflower seeds, baked in a moderate oven until lightly coloured

1 fresh red chilli, sliced and cut very thinly

1 tsp paprika

ground sea salt

1 Heat the vegetable oil to 170°C (330°F). Split the sweet potato into two batches, and fry the first batch in the hot oil, stirring all the time until crisp. This will take a few minutes. The potato slices must not burn – all you are doing is 'drying them out' in the oil, so to speak. When they stop sizzling, remove with a spatula.

2 Drain the slices and season lightly with salt. They will seem soft still, but will crisp up once cool. Wait for the oil to come back to the right temperature and repeat the process with the remaining sweet potato.

3 When the oil is hot again, add the chickpeas and cook at 180°C (350°F) until slightly shrivelled. Drain well.

4 Finally, add the chilli and cook for a few seconds to wilt and release its heat. Leave to drain with the chickpeas.

5 Let everything cool completely before placing all the ingredients in a bowl. Season well with ground sea salt and the paprika.

6 Nibble away to your heart's content.

Spicy Chicken and Pepper Pitta Pockets

Chicken thighs and drumsticks may be the cheapest cut of the bird, but they are also the tastiest. The secret is to cook the thighs first in a moderate oven – this way the flesh stays very soft and moist. You can also steam or poach the thighs first. It's really up to you.

4 chicken thighs, about 300 g/10 oz	2 tsp Thai green curry paste
1 onion, thinly sliced	3 tbsp freshly chopped coriander
1 yellow pepper, deseeded and cut into thin slices	3 tbsp freshly chopped parsley
	salt and freshly ground black pepper
4 tbsp grapeseed oil	4 pitta breads, sliced open into pockets

1 Roast the thighs in the oven at 160°C (325°F, Gas mark 3) for about 45 minutes, until soft and succulent. Remove the skin and pull the flesh away into bite-sized pieces.

2 Blanch the sliced onion and peppers in boiling salted water for 2 minutes. Drain well.

3 Heat the grapeseed oil in a wok, add the onion and peppers, and cook for 2 minutes. Add the chicken and Thai curry paste, and stir well. Season with salt and pepper, and add the coriander and parsley. Cook for a further 2–3 minutes.

4 Spoon into the warmed pittas and serve.

Pork and Chilli Burritos

Pork is the best meat to use in burritos. Having said that, I have eaten catfish burritos and also turkey varieties. Essentially, this is a peasant dish and benefits from long, slow cooking of cheaper cuts of meat. The point to remember is that it has to be spicy – this is offset by eating with sour cream and plenty of guacamole.

450 g/1 lb belly pork, free of skin and bone	3 cloves garlic, chopped
vegetable oil	1 tbsp chopped fresh red chilli
200 ml/7 fl oz strong chicken stock, boiling, plus 250 ml/8 fl oz extra	1 tsp ground cumin
	pinch of caster sugar
4 tbsp olive oil	2 tbsp red wine vinegar
1 small onion, chopped	6 tbsp freshly chopped coriander
1 red pepper, deseeded and finely chopped	salt and freshly ground black pepper
1 yellow pepper, deseeded and finely chopped	6 large flour tortillas

1 Place the belly pork in a frying pan with a little vegetable oil and brown well all over. Season well with salt and pepper.

2 Place in an ovenproof dish and cover with the 200 ml (7 fl oz) boiling stock. Cover with a tight-fitting lid and place in a preheated oven at 180°C (350°F, Gas mark 4) for 2 hours, or until very soft and tender.

3 Meanwhile, make the sauce. Heat the olive oil in a pan and add the onion, peppers, garlic, chilli, cumin and sugar, and cook over a high heat for 10 minutes to take a little colour.

4 Add the extra stock and vinegar, and season well. Bring to the boil and cook for a couple of minutes until slightly thickened. Now add the coriander and blend or process the whole lot until smooth.

5 Remove the cooked pork from the oven and chop very finely. Add enough of the sauce to moisten the pork well. Adjust the seasoning.

6 Fill each of the flour tortillas with the some pork sauce and wrap up well. Serve with sour cream, the rest of the sauce, pickled chillis and guacamole.

SERVES 4   PREP 20 MINS   COOK 10 MINS

Pan-fried Chicken Skewers with Tomato Relish

This is perfect kids' food, without all the fat that you get from a fast food chain.

4 medium skinless chicken breasts, cut into 2-cm/1-in cubes

4 tbsp plain flour

2 eggs, beaten

350 g/12 oz dry breadcrumbs

6 tsp vegetable oil

1 x 320 g/11 oz jar tomato relish

2 tsp dark soy sauce

2 tbsp tomato ketchup

2 tbsp Worcestershire sauce

250 ml/8 fl oz mayonnaise

4 tbsp freshly chopped coriander

salt and freshly ground black pepper

1 Skewer the chicken cubes onto 4 bamboo skewers. Season well with salt and pepper.

2 Place the flour, egg and breadcrumbs in three separate shallow bowls or plates.

3 Dust both sides of the chicken skewers in flour, dip in the beaten egg, then coat in breadcrumbs – pat down to make sure that the breadcrumbs have stuck and the chicken is more or less covered.

4 Heat a large frying pan or griddle pan. Add the vegetable oil and allow to heat, then add the chicken and cook gently for 5–6 minutes on each side, or until cooked through and nicely browned.

5 Meanwhile, stir together the relish, soy sauce, ketchup and Worcestershire sauce. Add the mayonnaise and coriander, and mix thoroughly. Season with salt and pepper.

6 Serve the chicken on a plate, with the relish spooned over the top.

Crumpet Pizza Toppings

Here are a couple of ideas if your kids don't eat pizzas. My kids won't touch pizza, so I devised this new approach and they love them. The choice is endless – just use a little imagination and see what happens. Crumpets are robust in their structure so hold up well to all flavourings and toppings.

Tomato and Cheddar Topping

8 round crumpets

2 x 400 g/13 oz tins chopped tomatoes in juice

1 small onion, very finely chopped

2 tbsp olive oil

2 tsp sugar

2 tsp vinegar

Cheddar cheese, grated

salt and freshly ground black pepper

Eggy Topping with Celery and Apple Slaw

8 square crumpets

4 large eggs, beaten

a little vegetable oil

6 tbsp reduced-fat mayonnaise

3 sticks celery, cut into matchsticks

2 green apples, cored, peeled and run through a mandolin

115 g/4 oz iceberg lettuce, finely shredded

lemon juice

freshly ground black pepper

1 To make the tomato and Cheddar topping, first grill or toast the crumpets.

2 Place all the ingredients except the cheese into a saucepan and gently cook until thick and stewlike. Season well with salt and pepper.

3 Spoon the topping onto the crumpets, top with the cheese and glaze in a hot oven or under the grill. Serve hot.

4 To make the eggy topping, dip the crumpets in the beaten egg.

5 Heat the vegetable oil in a frying pan, add the crumpets and cook for 3 minutes on each side. Keep warm.

6 Mix the mayonnaise, celery, apple and lettuce together with a squeeze of lemon juice and a little black pepper.

7 Pile onto the warm crumpets and serve.

Cauliflower Fritters with Sweet Chilli and Garlic Dipping Sauce

I really love cauliflower. The only problem is that it is a bit dull on its own and it overcooks really easily. Here it's matched with a very tasty chilli dip, which is a Chinese idea and works very well. A great starter or main course accompaniment to roast shoulder of lamb, roast duck or on its own as a vegetarian meal.

freshly grated zest and juice of 1 lemon	1 tsp sesame oil
1 small cauliflower, cut into small florets and blanched	2 eggs
	2 tbsp milk
3 tbsp sesame seeds	dry breadcrumbs
150 ml/5 fl oz Chinese sweet chilli sauce	vegetable oil for deep-frying
2 garlic cloves, crushed	salt and freshly ground black pepper

1 Place the lemon juice and zest in a bowl, add the cauliflower, season well and stir together. Leave to stand for about 30 minutes.

2 Meanwhile, make the dipping sauce. Place the sesame seeds on a baking sheet and toast under a preheated grill until golden. Place the seeds in a small bowl with the chilli sauce, garlic and sesame oil. Stir well and season.

3 Beat the eggs with the milk in a bowl, then dip in the cauliflower to coat well, shaking off any excess. Place one piece of cauliflower at a time in the breadcrumbs and toss so that they have a good coating. Repeat until all the cauliflower is coated.

4 Fill a deep fat-fryer or a deep pan one-third full of oil and heat to 165°C (330°F). Add the cauliflower and cook in the hot oil until golden brown. Remove from the oil and drain well on absorbent kitchen paper.

5 Pile the cauliflower up on a plate, with the sweet chilli sauce served separately for dipping.

Real Southern Fried Chicken with Hush Puppies

I spend a few weeks every year fishing in North Carolina with my good friend Cory, who also happens to be the chef at the very nice hotel in which I stay. This is an adaptation of one of his recipes. His Southern fried chicken is spot on and, on the rare occasions there are any leftovers, we take them with us for a picnic when we're fishing the next day! Hush puppies are another great standard from the Deep South and are perfect served with Iced Sweet Tea (page 130) and Real Southern Fried Chicken.

Real Southern Fried Chicken	Hush Puppies
55 g/2 oz dried oregano	150 g/5 oz finely ground cornmeal or polenta
55 g/2 oz dried thyme	150 g/5 oz self-raising flour
55 g/2 oz ground white pepper	3 pinches salt
125 g/4 oz plain flour	1 tbsp sugar
25 g/1 oz rock salt	1 tsp ground black pepper
4 eggs	1 medium egg
dash of Tabasco sauce	185 ml/6 fl oz buttermilk
4 chicken leg pieces	2 tbsp horseradish
vegetable oil for frying	3 spring onions, finely chopped
tomato relish and good-quality mayonnaise, to serve	vegetable oil for deep-frying
	mayonnaise, to serve

1 To make the fried chicken, finely grind the oregano and thyme together using a pestle and mortar, then mix with the ground white pepper, flour and rock salt in a large shallow dish or plate.

2 Beat the eggs together with 185 ml (6 fl oz) cold water. Strain the mixture through a sieve into another shallow dish and add the Tabasco.

3 Cut each chicken portion in half at the joint to give drumstick and thigh pieces. Toss the chicken in the flour and spice mixture to lightly dust, remove from the flour and place to one side. Dip each piece of chicken in the egg mixture, shake off any excess then put back into the flour mixture to coat – it's best to do this stage one piece at a time, otherwise you'll get very messy.

4 Heat some vegetable oil in a frying pan. Add the chicken pieces and fry for a few minutes on each side, or until golden brown – the oil should only come halfway up the sides of the chicken. Sit a wire cooling rack or grill pan grid securely on top of a roasting pan or baking tray, remove the browned chicken from the frying pan and arrange on the wire rack.

5 Bake in a preheated oven at 180°C (350°F, Gas mark 4) for 10–15 minutes, or until the chicken is cooked through. Remove from the oven and allow to rest for 15–20 minutes – I know they're tempting, but try to resist because they'll burn your mouth if you eat them straight away.

6 Meanwhile, make the hush puppies. Place the cornmeal, flour, salt, sugar and pepper in a bowl and mix well. Add the egg, buttermilk and horseradish, and mix well. Finally, add the spring onions. Cover and leave for 1 hour.

7 Heat the oil in a deep fat-fryer to 170°C (330°F) or fill a deep pan one-third full of oil and use a cooking thermometer to check the oil temperature. Spoon small amounts of the mixture into the hot oil and cook until golden brown. Remove from the hot oil and drain on absorbent kitchen paper.

8 The Americans eat their chicken plain, but I like to serve mine with tomato relish and mayonnaise. Eat warm, accompanied by the hush puppies dipped into a little mayonnaise. I like to drink sweet tea with lots of ice with both of these dishes. Dig in!

HINTS AND TIPS
- ► If you don't have a pestle and mortar to grind the dried herbs, tip them into a small bowl and use the end of a rolling pin to crush them. Alternatively, blitz them in a mini food processor.
- ► You can buy prepared chicken drumstick and thigh pieces if you don't want to joint the chicken legs yourself.

Baked Alaska

I really can't resist this – reminds me of my mum!

Sponge

3 large eggs, at room temperature

75 g/2¹/₂ oz caster sugar

75 g/2¹/₂ oz plain flour, sifted

25 g/1 oz unsalted butter, melted

1 x 410 g/13 oz tin peaches in syrup, drained

4 large egg whites, at room temperature

2 pinches cream of tartar

125 g/4 oz caster sugar, plus a little extra

125 g/4 oz icing sugar, sifted

squeeze of lemon juice

500 g/1 lb vanilla ice cream, softened but not sloppy

10 glacé cherries

125 g/4 oz angelica, cut into diamonds

¹/₂ orange, segments scooped out carefully and skin left intact

brandy

1 Lightly butter the inside of a 20 cm x 7 cm (8 in x 3 in) round cake tin. Chill until needed.

2 To make the sponge, place the eggs and caster sugar in a bowl and whip using an electric mixer until thick and foamy, so that the mixture holds its own weight. Remove from the machine and carefully fold in the flour and, finally, the melted butter.

3 Pour into the chilled sponge tin and cook in a preheated oven at 200°C (400°F, Gas mark 6) for 15 minutes, or until the sponge starts to shrink away from the side. Remove from the oven and cool, turn out of the tin and slice in half horizontally. Increase the oven temperature to 230°C (450°F, Gas mark 8).

4 Place the bottom half of the sponge on an ovenproof plate. Arrange the peaches over the top and drizzle over a little of the syrup.

5 Whisk the egg whites with the cream of tartar at medium speed until thick and foamy. Add the 125 g (4 oz) caster sugar and whisk again on a low speed until thick and glossy. Remove the bowl from the machine. Fold in the icing sugar and lemon.

6 Place the ice cream on top of the peaches and top with the second piece of sponge. Spoon half of the meringue onto the sponge and seal very quickly. Smooth with a palette knife.

7 Place the rest of meringue into a large Savoy piping bag fitted with a 1 cm (1/2 in) fluted nozzle. Pipe a nice design over the cake, then decorate with the glacé cherries and angelica.

8 Place the orange half-skin on top and stick into the meringue carefully, but not too far. Sprinkle with a little extra caster sugar. Place in the hot oven for 2–3 minutes to brown lightly.

9 Remove from the oven and heat a little brandy in a ladle and pour into the orange. Light and 'Hey, presto!'

10 Cut into large wedges and serve with double cream

SERVES
4

PREP
20
MINS

COOK
2
HOURS

Marinated Strawberries with Almond Meringue

People may sneer, but the bought packet meringue is actually very good. The other point to mention is that it keeps indefinitely, so you can always keep it in the cupboard ready to go. Simple meringue that tastes sensational with strawberries.

1 x 275 g/9 oz packet meringue mix

1 tsp grated nutmeg

25 g/1 oz unrefined granulated sugar

100 g/3¹/₂ oz flaked almonds, lightly browned in the oven

450 g/1 lb English strawberries, hulled and halved

juice and finely grated zest of 1 large lemon

finely grated zest of 1 orange

4 tbsp unrefined icing sugar

thick or lightly whipped double cream, to serve

1 Line two baking sheets with nonstick baking parchment.

2 Place the meringue mix, nutmeg and sugar into a mixing bowl and whisk at a high speed until thick and glossy – this will take about 10 minutes. Remove the bowl from the machine and fold in the almonds.

3 Using a large, wetted serving spoon (not a tablespoon), scoop out large 'dollops' of the meringue and place on the baking sheet. Try to keep a nice tail to the top of the meringue dollops and leave a nice gap between each one. Bake in a preheated oven at 140°C (275°F, Gas mark 1) for 2 hours to dry out and colour slightly – they should still be a little gooey inside.

4 Meanwhile, wash and halve the strawberries and place in a bowl. Add the lemon juice, lemon and orange zests and icing sugar, then mix well. Cover and leave at room temperature for the length of time it takes to cook the meringue, stirring occasionally.

5 To serve, spoon the strawberries into deep bowls and top with a meringue. Drizzle a little double cream over the top.

Angel Cake with Mango and Custard

All kids love the taste and texture of angel cake. I adored it as a child, but here we add a little fruit surreptitiously in the form of tinned mango. Fresh mangoes are fine, if a little expensive and sometimes not too ripe, so we always keep a tin on hand in the cupboard.

---

1 x 200 g/7 oz tin mango slices, drained

1 shop-bought angel cake, sliced into 4 chunks

a few raspberries

2 x small tubs low-fat custard (about 100g/3½ oz each)

chocolate or coloured sprinkles or edible silver decoration balls, to decorate

---

1 Lay the mango slices in the bottom of 4 bowls.

2 Place the sponge on top, then sprinkle over a few raspberries, finally spoon over the cold custard and dot with a few 'sprinkles' or silver balls.

3 Serve. Who said kids' food is not delicious?

Classic Banana Split

A real classic pud, in the late 1960s and 1970s the banana split was the dessert to have in posh restaurants. I love this pudding!

4 ripe bananas, halved lengthways	ready-made bitter chocolate sauce
good-quality vanilla ice cream	225 ml/8 fl oz very lightly
12 walnut halves, crushed	whipped double cream
250 g/8 oz ready-made fresh	4 glacé cherries
raspberry sauce	edible silver decoration balls

1 Place the bananas in 4 glass serving dishes and add 2 or 3 balls of vanilla ice cream to each one.

2 Sprinkle over the walnuts.

3 Spoon over equal amounts of chocolate and raspberry sauce.

4 Finally, pipe or spoon over the double cream and top each banana split with a glacé cherry and silver balls.

Index